RETURN ‗TO‗ CENTER

52 WEEKLY STRATEGIES FOR PEACE, STRENGTH, AND JOY

RETURN ᵀᴼ CENTER

52 WEEKLY STRATEGIES FOR PEACE, STRENGTH, AND JOY

JULIET MADISON

ixia
PRESS

Garden City, New York

This Ixia Press edition is a new work, first published by Dover Publications in 2025.

Library of Congress Cataloging-in-Publication Data

Names: Madison, Juliet, author.
Title: Return to center: 52 weekly strategies for peace, strength, and joy / [Juliet Madison].
Description: Ixia Press edition. | Garden City, New York: Ixia Press, [2025] | "This Ixia Press edition is a new work, first published by Dover Publications in 2025." | Summary: "Connect to your inner core, cultivate positivity, resilience, and fulfillment, and find the calm you crave, one week at a time, with 52 weeks of 'centering' techniques and practical strategies"—Provided by publisher.
Identifiers: LCCN 2024025346 | ISBN 9780486852652 (trade paperback)
Subjects: LCSH: Self-actualization (Psychology) | Body-mind centering. | Self-help techniques.
Classification: LCC BF637.S4 M2245 2024 | DDC 158.1/28—dc23/eng/20240805
LC record available at https://lccn.loc.gov/2024025346

Publisher: Betina Cochran
Senior Acquisitions Editor: Fiona Hallowell
Managing Editorial Supervisor: Susan Rattiner
Production Editor: Gregory Koutrouby
Cover Designer: Mark Voss
Creative Manager: Marie Zaczkiewicz
Interior Designer: Robyn Kamholtz
Production: Pam Weston, Tammi McKenna, Ayse Yilmaz

IXIA PRESS
An imprint of Dover Publications

Printed in China
85265201   2024
www.doverpublications.com/ixiapress

CONTENTS

                                                                    PAGE

Introduction vii
How to Get the Most Out of This Book xi

 1. Get to Know Your Center 1
 2. Verbal Commands 4
 3. The Joy List 6
 4. The Next 30 Minutes 9
 5. Your Foundation 12
 6. Stop 15
 7. Color Immersion 17
 8. Move Your Energy 19
 9. Rebirth Yourself 21
10. Flip the Switch 24
11. A Different Approach 27
12. Feel-Good Playlist 30
13. The Continuum 32
14. Sacred Spaces 35
15. What Would It Take? 37
16. Morning Ms 39
17. Reframe 41
18. Pull Back 44
19. Appreciate 46
20. Wanting & Giving 48
21. Quote It 51
22. Animal Instinct 53

23. Rituals 55

24. Find Your Rhythm 58

25. Ask Your Guides 60

26. Let Go 63

27. Crystallize 66

28. Trust Your Truth 68

29. Magic Mirror 71

30. Centering Sequence 74

31. Random Guidance 76

32. Emotional First Aid Kit 78

33. Centering Jewelry 81

34. Physical Considerations 83

35. The Message 87

36. Stepping to Center 91

37. Totality 94

38. Explore 98

39. Verbalize 101

40. Remember the Ocean .104

41. Nothing Needs to Be Fixed 106

42. Rapid Reset 109

43. Mother Yourself 112

44. Center Poem 115

45. Make a Decision 118

46. Moments, Not Minutes 122

47. Silence and Stillness 126

48. Naturalize 131

49. Choices 134

50. Choose a State of Being 137

51. Draw and Color Your Center 140

52. Center Vision 142

INTRODUCTION

Our center is that core part of ourselves where healing, hope, and harmony resides. It's the nonphysical, unseen, innately felt sense of power and peace; an energetic place where the true source of our self exists without any faults, illnesses, or requirements. It is our pure essence, and is connected to the essence of all others and to the Earth and universe itself; a unified link between all living things.

Consciously choosing to be centered is the ultimate in self-care. It's about being tuned in to your core self, your true spiritual nature, where there is no judgment, no pain, and no fear. For want of a better explanation, it's like heaven on the inside. It feels balanced, it feels peaceful, it feels confident, it feels well. It's knowing you can say "I've got this" no matter what is going on. Regardless of your religious beliefs or culture, we all have this inner core, this soul part of ourselves where our true, unlimited nature resides, and is not only part of us but part of *all* of us; together, united, as a whole. By being centered yourself, you also help others to more easily return to their center too.

Centering is the foundation of peace, alignment, and manifestation. It tunes us in to our source, which is love, and shines a light on our authentic self so that we are supported throughout any challenge and allowed to be the best and happiest version of ourselves.

Returning to center works from the inside out. Instead of trying to fix all the things you cannot control in an attempt to feel better about your life, you aim to feel better on the inside *first* so that it doesn't matter as much what is going on around you. And do you know what often happens when you are centered and aligned on the inside? The outside circumstances often shift anyway, seemingly by themselves! Our true power is not in influencing things around us, but by returning to ourselves, which allows the power of the universe to manage all those external things. This is not to say that you shouldn't take external action, or make changes; it is simply to emphasize where your true power lies. And when you know this, everything else is work-out-able.

Throughout any challenge, you CAN feel centered, grounded, and at peace. It may not be one hundred percent of the time, and that is okay. But you can have centered moments, and the more you practice these strategies, the more of those moments you'll have. If you feel overwhelmed, exhausted, frustrated, time-poor, tired or unwell—if you feel held back from your goals and dreams, feel that no one understands you, or feel too sensitive to handle modern life—centering can help. It's not about hiding your feelings, or being positive all the time—feelings *should* be experienced and expressed. It's about having a continual connection to that special part of you, that *center*, that holds you up despite everything you go through.

A few years ago, I had surgery to remove a vital organ after ten years of illness. During my recovery, I began receiving flashes of inspiration and insight, not really knowing what it was. I thought at first I was simply journaling; jotting down thoughts and words to help me through a challenging time when my physical capabilities were limited but my mind was active. But these words seemed to come *through* me, not *from* me.

As the words kept coming effortlessly and I found myself not even having to think about what I was writing, I realized I was channeling insight and guidance from. . . somewhere. Perhaps the collective universal consciousness that ties us all together. It felt similar to the process of doing intuitive readings and coaching for my clients around the world, where I tap into their energy and pinpoint areas of significance or answer their burning questions. But this time I was reading myself, at first.

As these insights began to help me regain my sense of peace, I realized they could help others too. When I decided to consciously open myself up to receiving more insight, it flowed even more, and in a way that I felt I was tapping into a universal need; a core, unified link between us all that requires nourishment and support, a center within ourselves, and within the Earth and universe itself, that we can sometimes stray from during life, but that *can* be accessed and returned to. We *can* return to this center of stability.

I didn't consciously sit down to create and write these strategies. I waited for each to come to me organically, which they did regularly, mostly at night while I was lying in bed—or more accurately, sitting in bed, as my recovery required me to sleep semi-upright! And this book, which was first an online course, is the result. What started as a way for me to cope with a challenging time, soon became a way for me to reach others with their own unique challenges, goals, and dreams, united by our spirit and human need for connection and peace within ourselves. The strategies also became extremely helpful when I was later diagnosed with PTSD, and then went on to experience a long struggle with infertility, recurrent miscarriages, and the roller coaster of IVF. Life is not without challenges, but it is also not without the power to navigate through them with strength we often don't know we have until it's needed.

Centering is an ongoing journey, not a destination. It is an active practice to integrate into your life, just as you integrate exercise, meditation, social experiences, and recreation.

When you are centered, you are enjoying all the benefits that come from being in a state of:

- *Love*
- *Balance*
- *Truth*
- *Peace*
- *Awareness*
- *Knowing*
- *Acceptance*
- *Authenticity*
- *Healing*
- *Clarity*
- *Purpose*
- *Strength*
- *Alignment*

With these aspects in place, our inner experience and perspective are joyful and positive, and this has a ripple effect to our outer experiences, helping our lives become more joyful and harmonious.

When you're centered, manifestations happen more quickly and easily, too, and in alignment with your true self and what is best for you, because you're operating from the highest vibration of yourself. When you're in this state, everything that happens is right for you. Everything. Even the challenges. Centering allows you not to be afraid of challenges that are a normal part of life, but to know that all is well in the big picture.

In life, people often want the great career, the amazing partner, the perfect holiday, the house, good health and longevity, the book deal, the lotto win, etc., because it's normal and human to desire things that we think will make us feel good. But what if you could feel good, or better, regardless of what you have or don't have? And what if by feeling better within *first*, those things you want come to you more easily?

This is what *can* happen, and *often* happens.

This is the power of RETURNING TO CENTER.

Juliet

HOW TO GET THE MOST
OUT OF THIS BOOK

✳ You might choose to read this book from beginning to end and absorb the content first, or you may choose to read one chapter or strategy each day or week, integrating the suggested activities into your life a week at a time.

✳ You might also like to turn to a random page and focus on that particular strategy first, doing the activities in any order you like. If you choose this option, start with the first chapter, which gives you a foundational awareness of your center to assist with all the other strategies.

✳ You might like to team up with a friend and go through the book via a buddy system, with each of you going through the material together and sharing your responses and experiences.

✳ You could start a Return to Center support circle or book club with a group of people, either in person or online, and read a chapter at a time, participating in and sharing your experience of the strategies, while providing support and encouragement to others on the same journey.

✳ While reading through the book, you could bookmark certain pages or activities that you'd like to delve further into with the help of a professional, and ask them to assist you in a way that best suits your individual circumstances and needs.

✳ If at any time you feel unable to cope or gain benefit from the strategies, please reach out to an understanding friend or family member, a health professional, or a helpline, and always remember that support is out there and you can and will feel better again.

✳ Share your experiences of the strategies or feedback about the book on social media with the hashtag #returntocenterbook and tag me on Instagram at @julietmadisonauthorartist and Facebook at @julietmadisonauthor

RETURN TO CENTER

52 WEEKLY STRATEGIES FOR PEACE, STRENGTH, AND JOY

1

GET TO KNOW YOUR CENTER

B ring your center to life through sensory detail, so that you have an awareness of this space within you that you can refer to. Because your center is not a physical area like a part of your body, you need to tune in more intuitively to discover or create what this space looks like or feels like to you.

Some people are more visual, while others might be more tuned in to another sense like touch or sound, so you might find that one sense overtakes the others, or you might find that it's fairly balanced. There's no right or wrong way. What matters is that you get an energetic picture of your center in whatever form works for you.

Try to create a visual image of your center or a sense of how it feels so you can see it or visit it any time you like.

What does it look like? Is it a room, or a garden, or just a swirling ball of light or color? Is it indefinable but you can see various elements such as a flower, a soft cushion, a fluffy cloud, or a supportive hand?

Don't judge what you see, just accept it and allow your inner eye to roam around and notice anything that looks like it belongs in your center. It's like home decorating from within, because you are your home, your center is your home, and you can have anything you like in there.

If you have trouble, see if anything is dulling, diminishing, or covering this center, preventing you from fully connecting. Perhaps it is too dark to see? Too blurry? Are there obstacles in the way, such as a fence around it or a door you can't open?

I had closed off my heart many years ago to avoid feeling painful emotions and memories. I was at a seminar where they did a visualization exercise to see what our heart looked and felt like on the inside. All I could see was a splintery wooden cage around my heart. I hadn't realized until that moment how much I had closed it off. The image was so vivid that tears started falling down my face, and it was as though I could physically feel this cage within; splinters sticking into my heart, and outward, too, preventing anyone getting close, and hiding my true self. There was a light inside but it couldn't get out. It couldn't expand. I was unable to continue with the rest of this seminar due to the intense emotions I was experiencing as all my hurt and past trauma came to the surface. However painful it was, this awareness through visualization was an important first step for me in opening my heart again. Over time, I tore away those splintery shards of aged timber around my heart and let the universe carry them away so my heart could glow and expand again.

Now my heart is so open it can sometimes feel overwhelming, but instead of hiding it away in a cage, I like to imagine wrapping it in a soft, comforting blanket for extra support during emotional times.

Tune in to see if anything is in the way of connecting with your heart or your center. If there is, describe it, write it down, so you can take steps to remove it. You might like to do a meditation and visualization, imagining the barrier being dissolved by white light, or seeing it being picked apart by a helping hand and thrown into the universe for disposal. Seek professional assistance if it seems too difficult to manage on your own.

Otherwise, continue visualizing your center, and now bring in the other senses as well.

If your center had a texture, what would it would feel like? Is it like soft, lush grass, comforting fluffy carpet, or smooth, polished timber like a dance floor? Are there any other tactile sensations?

What sounds resonate with your center? Birds, classical music, a particular theme song, flowing water, or simply silence?

Do any scents or tastes come to mind?

Also notice any words that describe your center: inviting, sacred, secure, comforting, free, warm or cool, etc.

By describing your center, you will find it easier to do other centering techniques and have a place to visit during meditation or during challenging moments in your life.

And remember, your center is not an escape. It is not a place to run away to or hide or distract yourself from life. It is a pure connection point where your true power resides.

ACTIVITY

Using the space below or a separate journal, describe your center in as much sensory detail as possible using the guidelines on the previous page. It doesn't have to be written beautifully or in any kind of order. It can be key words jotted down, a mind map, sketches and drawings, symbols, words, song lyrics, etc.

Over the next week, consciously tune in to your center as often as you can, drawing upon the sensory detail you came up with. The more you do so, the richer it will become, and the easier it will be to return to when needed.

_____

_____

_____

_____

_____

_____

_____

_____

_____

_____

_____

_____

_____

2

VERBAL COMMANDS

Our thoughts are powerful, and so are our spoken words. Make the most of this by consciously stating your requests out loud—in this case, the desire to return to center. Say to yourself as often as needed, "Return to center." Even when you're nowhere near center, and possibly teetering on the edge of existence, simply ask, "Help me return to center," then surrender and flow with the process. There is always support around you and you need only ask for it.

Sometimes simply saying these words will get you there in a flash. And the more you practice it, the easier it gets. Other times you'll need to take more specific action, physically and/or mentally (using other tips in this book).

Here's another option: When you catch yourself thinking or repeating negative thoughts or limiting beliefs, or dwelling in uncomfortable emotions, say the word "CLEAR" or "CANCEL," and imagine those thoughts or emotions being sucked away into an energetic vacuum cleaner or deleted on a computer. Then breathe and change your thinking, replacing it with the thought you now choose or the new belief you want to install.

The more you do this, the more you will become aware of even a slight straying from your center, and the easier it is to get back. Also, by doing this you are actually rewiring your brain to cope better with stress, and retraining an emotionally reactive part of your brain called the amygdala to help you get out of a downward spiral of negative thoughts or fear and move into a healthier and calmer state of mind.

So any time you become aware of unhelpful thoughts or emotions, or you can't seem to get out of a funk, try a verbal command of your choice. Keep saying it with conviction any time it's needed, even if it's one hundred times a day at first, until it starts to become second nature. Your mind will learn to automatically summon the word subconsciously whenever it detects thoughts or perceptions that are not serving you.

Start with "Cancel" or "Clear!" and then say, "Return to Center." Take a deep breath, and if you like, visualize your center or an aspect of it that helps you feel peaceful and comforted.

ACTIVITY

Try a verbal command as often as possible throughout the following week and see how it goes. If you forget, you might like to set a daily reminder or periodic reminders throughout the day to check in with yourself, and just say, "Return to center" if needed.

CANCEL unhelpful thoughts

CLEAR your energy

RETURN TO CENTER

3

THE JOY LIST

This is one of my favorite activities for connecting to my center.

Make a list of things that make you feel centered, happy, and joyful. Those simple pleasures and big pleasures that you love experiencing. Things that make you feel like YOU.

But don't just write a list from top to bottom on a page in your journal (though you can start with this if you like in order to brainstorm and get clarity on your wording). Get a piece of blank paper or cardboard (or use a double page in your journal) and make a work of art out of it. Don't worry if you don't consider yourself artistic, it's not a painting or anything fancy. It's just a special way of writing a list and creating something beautiful to display on a wall if you wish.

This activity is great for raising your vibration and moving back into your center, and giving you some ideas of things to do to feel good when you need it. It's also great for helping you on the road to discovering your purpose, or creating your purpose, because a purpose is what you decide it to be. Your purpose doesn't have to be anything grand, unless you want it to be. It can be as simple as seeing the beauty in everyone and everything. Or, it can mean being creative. Don't confuse purpose with a career. For example, my purpose is not to write books and courses. It is to entertain and inspire others. My writing is just one tool I like to use to achieve or embrace that purpose.

So start with your Joy List and see where else it leads. It may awaken hidden passions or help clarify your purpose. When you return to joy, you return to your center.

Here are some examples of things that bring me joy, to give you an idea.

- *Watching clouds float in the sky*
- *Long hugs*
- *Hot chocolate*
- *Going to the movies*
- *Making art*
- *A good belly laugh*
- *Listening to guided meditations*
- *Taking photos of flowers*
- *Reading inspirational quotes*
- *Writing stories*
- *Funny memes*
- *Walking along the beach*
- *Cuddling cats*
- *Watching sunsets*
- *Positive conversations*
- *Browsing in beautiful shops*
- *TV & movie blooper reels*

ACTIVITY: Making Your Joy List

Gather some materials including paper, cardboard, or your journal, and a fancy pen or colored markers. Use the heading, Things That Bring Me Joy.

You could write the heading in the middle of the paper with a circle around it and then write each item at various angles around it, like a mind map. Or you could write it all as a spiral from the middle; or from left to right then turning the paper horizontally and writing left to right again until you reach the center. It could also be a simple top-to-bottom continuous list with a dot between each item, writing until you fill up the page. Play around with different ways to lay out your words. You may like to practice in your journal before making the "official" list. You can also add little drawings or sketches, doodles, symbols, or even stickers—whatever feels joyful.

When complete, display it somewhere you'll see it regularly, and take a photo to save it, perhaps as a screensaver or phone lock screen. Have fun!

To help get you started, jot down three to five things here that bring you joy:

1. _____

_____

2. _____

_____

3. _____

_____

4. _____

_____

5. _____

_____

4

THE NEXT 30 MINUTES

When life is overwhelming, think only of your next 30 minutes. What do you need to do in the next thirty minutes ONLY? What is your next best step? What do you *want* to do? Is there something you *have* to do? Or can the next 30 minutes be about doing nothing and just *being*? Will you take a shower or bath, go for a walk, or do another centering activity? When the 30 minutes are up, only then think about what's next. You will be in a better place mentally to handle whatever you need to going forward.

When we think too far ahead or multitask, we can lose sight of the present moment and decrease our productivity and our satisfaction. It's still good to have a plan and know as much as possible about what is coming up, but then step back and be in the moment. When you divide the awareness of your time into 30-minute segments, it feels manageable, but also long enough to make progress with something or enjoy a peaceful bit of time out. Even if you plan to do something in particular for the next two hours, still try to segment your awareness into half-hour chunks, and set an intention for each chunk that allows you to be fully present and focused on what you are doing.

Examples:

✳ *"For the next 30 minutes I will do nothing but write my story—no editing or research or distractions, just writing."*

✳ *"For the next 30 minutes I will enjoy a long, hot shower followed by massaging my favorite body lotion into my skin."*

✳ *"For the next 30 minutes I will sit in nature and notice all the pleasing sights, sounds, and scents."*

✳ *"For the next 30 minutes I will read a book and not look at my phone."*

✳ *"For the next 30 minutes I will answer emails and messages."*
✳ *"For the next 30 minutes I will declutter parts of my house."*

Depending on the activity, stop after 30 minutes and reassess. Decide whether to continue, or to start a new 30-minute segment.

Set a timer if it will help, or a gentle automatic reminder. In some jobs or situations it may not be possible to segment your awareness or activities completely, but any time you remember this tip, simply check the time and consciously choose what your focus will be for the next 30 minutes, even if it's just focusing on smiling at as many people as possible, or relaxing your muscles, or breathing more fully, or appreciating things around you while you go about your daily tasks.

I find this strategy incredibly helpful, both as a general way to make productive use of time and as a self-help strategy for days when everything feels too difficult. Sometimes I feel like I can't handle a whole day or week of my To Do list, but I CAN handle 30 minutes. So that's what I focus on.

ACTIVITY

Give this technique a try every day for the next week and notice how much more in control and centered you feel. You might like to write down some 30-minute segment ideas that you can use throughout the week, depending on your upcoming schedule or plans, like the examples above. What are some activities you could segment into 30-minute chunks of time?

_____

_____

_____

5

YOUR FOUNDATION

Everything that needs to stand strong and withstand daily life, like buildings, cars, roads, etc., needs to have a strong foundation. Without it, they won't last, or they will be prone to damage.

It's the same for us. We need a strong foundation in order to thrive. Physically we have our skeleton and the rest of what makes up our bodies to withstand living on Earth, but what about emotionally? What is our emotional foundation? What is it that helps us to stay in our center or return to it more easily?

Decide what is important to you, what is essential for your own well-being, and make this the foundation of your daily life. Think of this as your emotional scaffolding—the things that hold you up emotionally.

I wrote a foundation list when I was recovering from surgery and struggling to cope. I figured that if I could at least have my basic foundational needs met I could handle things better, but first, I had to find out what they were. One of them was 8–9 hours of sleep, but I wasn't getting it. I knew that if I was feeling tired or upset, then this could be contributing to my sense of feeling overwhelmed, so I chose to work on taking steps to maximize my sleep. I also had a need for a nap or deep meditation each afternoon, and I found on the days when I didn't get that, I didn't cope as well. So I worked on making sure that any days spent out and about included an option for some stillness or time out to rest in between activities, even if this meant laying the car seat back and resting in a parking lot for a while.

I also discovered that another foundational need was being able to talk about or express how I was feeling—not to dwell on anything negative, but to acknowledge and honor my feelings and feel heard. If I got upset because I felt no one was listening or I didn't feel understood, I realized I had to fulfill this foundational need in some way, by either asking someone if they would be able to provide an ear to just listen to me without trying to fix anything, or by writing my feelings down in a letter to the universe.

By knowing what your emotional foundation is, you can better help yourself. You can also show this list to your partner, family, or close friends so that they can be aware of what your needs are and be a support when you need it.

Some other examples that contribute to your foundation might be:

* *Spending some time outdoors each day*
* *Drinking enough water*
* *Not going more than 2 hours without eating*
* *Having a short nap each afternoon*
* *Writing down a gratitude list each night*
* *Having a time limit for how long you scroll through social media*
* *Doing daily stretches*
* *Reading something positive each morning like a motivational quote*
* *Switching off and winding down for bed by 10 pm*
* *Not responding to every message immediately, doing things at the times that are right for you*

These things are a bit different from your Joy List, though there might be some overlap. Keep your foundation list fairly brief, with no more than 3–6 items. Try to think only of the *essential* things you need for emotional stability; to feel good and feel like yourself each day, both physically and emotionally. Other things are more like a bonus. As an example: foundational needs for a house include a floor, walls, a roof, and doors/windows. The house needs to be built with materials that withstand the weather, and connected by strong joinery to hold it together. This is the foundation. Curtains, carpet, lighting, furniture, and decorations are bonuses. The house will still survive without these things. When creating your foundation, think what is important to hold you together, which may be different from what someone else needs. You may need lots of quiet time alone each day to do your own thing, process your feelings, and have your own space, whereas someone else may need regular company, interaction, and conversation to feel emotionally stable. You may need music each day to feel good, whereas another person may prefer silence or the sounds of nature.

ACTIVITY

In your journal or below, create a list of at least three of your foundational needs. And then, any time you're feeling uncentered or confused as to why you're feeling a certain way, check your list. Are any of your essentials not being tended to? Anything out of balance? If so, tend to those things to return to center.

If all the essentials are covered but you're still feeling off-center, then that is when a stronger re-centering activity is needed.

Use the following week to set, rebuild, or strengthen your foundation.

_____

_____

_____

_____

_____

_____

_____

_____

_____

_____

6

STOP

Stop for half an hour, ten minutes, one minute, even just ten seconds to take a long, deep, delicious breath, and calm your whole nervous system down. Do it now. Do it as long as you can or wish. The world will still go on. It will be okay without your attention on it for a while. In fact, it will be even better off after you've taken your attention away and focused only on your breath, because you will be better off for doing so, and when you feel better the world feels better.

STOP and feel your breath filling your lungs.
STOP and sense your heartbeat keeping you alive.
STOP and become aware of your presence where you are right now.
You are a miracle.
You are a masterpiece.
You are love expressed in physical form.
STOP and feel this magnificence that is you, and know that all is well.

There are four ways to incorporate "stopping" into your life:

1. Take a STOP day where you remove your attention from the ongoing issues of the world or in your life, and focus only on slowing down, pausing, stopping, or doing something out of the ordinary in which you don't allow any outside influences to take up physical, mental, and emotional space. Turn off your phone or put it on silent (tell loved ones you'll be off the radar for the day), and let your soul guide your day.

2. STOP whenever you think of it, and just focus on your breathing.

3. Put sticky notes or dot stickers in different places around your home or workplace, and when you see them, use it as a reminder to STOP for a moment.

4. Punctuate your daily tasks by stopping fully between them. See each task as a segment of your life (such as with The Next 30 Minutes strategy), and STOP between segments. Allow yourself to return to center before moving onto your next task so you are refreshed for each activity, instead of letting one thing carry over to the next and diluting your focus and energy.

The world won't stop for you (although in some ways it took a few STOP breaks itself during the pandemic). You have to do it yourself and take control in this fast-paced, busy world we live in. Stop and find your peace, and return to center.

ACTIVITY

Decide how you will incorporate **STOP** moments or days into your life. Schedule them into your calendar now, or set reminders on your phone, but also practice becoming aware of times throughout your day when you can use this strategy. Write down a few ideas below.

_____

_____

_____

_____

_____

_____

7

COLOR IMMERSION

Close your eyes and take a few deep breaths, and feel the existence of your center. See with your mind's eye, or even better, your heart's eye, a color. It may be your favorite color, or a different color may pop into your awareness. What color do you need right now to feel centered? Color has energy, too, and the power to shift our emotions.

When you've chosen a color (it could be basic like red or blue, or more specific like watermelon or aqua or mint green), look around your immediate environment and see if you can notice that color anywhere. Even better, now or sometime this week immerse yourself in this color for at least 10–30 minutes by consciously looking for that color around you wherever you are, or look in a shop, a garden or nursery, at the gym, a café, etc. Take photos anywhere you see this color if you like, to record your color immersion experience.

Then look for and notice that color here and there throughout the next week. Keep a journal with you or use your phone and jot down what you see; what the object or source of the color is, how it makes you feel, any ideas or memories it brings.

You may even like to continue this activity for the whole month, with the same color or with a different color each week.

This is also a great way to shift your focus away from the overstimulation from negative things on the news or social media, to remind you to be in the present and tuned in to the simple beauty around you.

Another fun way to do a color immersion is with the "Pinterest" app or website. Search for the name of your color and see what shows up, and save the images you're drawn to in a new Pinterest board just for that color. You can also refine your search by searching for specific items in that color such as flowers, cars, houses, dresses, handbags, sunsets, candles, books, etc. I've made an aqua board and a pink board. Just looking through the images I saved in these boards makes me feel happy and more centered.

You might even like to flip through magazines or print pictures and make a color board by gluing them onto cardboard or in your notebook. Have some creative fun with it!

ACTIVITY

Choose a color and try some of the techniques in this chapter. Look for the color around you wherever you go, or create a Pinterest board. You will find that the more you consciously choose to see this color, the more of it you will see, even when you're not actively looking. That is the law of attraction showing you what you choose to focus on. For example: when I did this activity once, I chose the color yellow. After I made my decision, I checked some messages online, and a friend I had been in contact with on Messenger had just changed the color of the chat screen to yellow.

8

MOVE YOUR ENERGY

Ask your brain to move your fingers.
Then your toes.
Ask your mouth to smile.
See how amazing that is? That's life force energy coursing through you, creating nerve impulses, responding instantly to your mind's direction. You are a powerful being of energy and choice.

Ask your body to move around in a way that pleases you. Don't think, just move intuitively. Whether you jump on the spot, jiggle, dance like Fred Astaire or Michael Jackson, or sway in slow motion, it doesn't matter. Move in a way that feels good right now, in this moment. Doesn't that feel better?

Let your energy move and flow to release blockages and emotions and allow fresh, new positive energy to flow through you. Keep the energy from your center flowing—don't block the flow.

Every now and again, or during difficult emotional times, ask, "How does my body need to move right now?"

It's well known that simply going for a walk can improve your mood, and that may be all you feel like doing, but with this exercise try to move in a more unique, centered way, from your soul. Feel into your center, then move.

It doesn't have to look good, be rhythmic, or make any sense, it only has to help you feel like energy is moving through your body in the way that you choose, at a speed that you decide. If all you feel like moving is a few fingers or your hand, then that's fine, and if you feel like jumping on the bed and waving your arms about exuberantly then that is fine too.

ACTIVITY

Do this a few times this week, or each morning when you get out of bed, or each afternoon to help wake you up and move into the next part of your day in a more centered way. Reflect on the following: How did the movement feel to you? Did it feel like it released any emotions, or brought up any issues? You may wish to journal about what came up for you. If you're feeling brave or curious, you may even wish to record your movements on video so you can watch it and see what comes up.

How do YOU need to move right now?

_____

_____

_____

_____

_____

_____

_____

_____

_____

_____

9

REBIRTH YOURSELF

Going through an emotional journey is like the birth process. It hurts, and it can take a while, but it's going to happen whether we like it or not, and the only way through it is through it. And, the outcome is almost always completely worth the pain. We become a new version of ourselves; we effectively *give birth* to ourselves.

Whatever you are feeling right now, allow yourself to feel it.

Feel it as a passing experience, like childbirth, moving through something uncomfortable or uncertain to release it and allow for something new to be born.

Remember, "passage not permanence," when it comes to difficult emotions. Let them through, let them pass, and feel the relief when they are out of you. Emotion is e-motion: energy in motion.

The previous chapter discussed moving your energy physically. In this chapter you'll be moving your *emotional* energy. Carve out some privacy and quiet for yourself, now or sometime in the next couple of days. Sit with your journal and allow yourself to feel whatever you are feeling. Feel it, and if you wish, write it. Don't be afraid of what comes up; let it through, and let it pass. Then go and do something from the Joy List chapter to help shift your vibration and get back to your day.

If you like, try doing some emotional journaling a few days this week, or every night before bed. Get used to *feeling* and *acknowledging*, and *knowing* that this is part of your rebirth, part of your journey to a more connected and joyful relationship with your center.

Your emotions don't have to be negative or challenging. You may be feeling pretty amazing right now, or you may be feeling like you're on a roller coaster. Whatever you feel, feel it and write about it.

ACTIVITY

To explore your emotions more deeply and assist with your rebirthing, try some of these journaling prompts:

* *What are three emotions I'm feeling right now?*

* *Where in my body are these feelings stored, or most concentrated? (You don't have to be able to feel this physically. Trust your intuition as to where the emotion is focusing itself: heart, lower back, ankle, liver, ears, lips.)*

* *What is one main recurring emotion or emotional pattern? (Frustration, abandonment, struggle, disbelief, being misunderstood).*

* *If I could choose how to feel, I would feel:*

* *What message does my main emotion have for me? What is it trying to tell me?*

* *What does my main emotion need or want right now? (Rest, self-expression, movement, salt water, vitamins, laughter, a massage, nature.)*

10

FLIP THE SWITCH

Are there common emotions or themes that come up when you are not feeling fully centered? For example: feeling alone, misunderstood, or frustrated? Or perhaps lost, purposeless, or unfulfilled?

Remember, it's okay to feel what you're feeling. Emotion is energy in motion and it needs to move and pass through in order to be transformed or to allow new emotion to be born, as in the process of your rebirth. And rebirth isn't necessarily a one-off occurrence. You can undergo this process many times, over months or years, sometimes even in one day. We are constantly evolving—emotionally and spiritually.

So how can you help this process along? How can you get closer to the light at the end of the tunnel and become more centered?

You can allow things to evolve at their own pace, but you can also Flip the Switch.

In other words, find where you're at emotionally and consciously make the switch from one state to another. For example:

* *Fear to LOVE*
* *Head to HEART*
* *Obligation to CHOICE*
* *Past to PRESENT*
* *Overwhelmed to CALM*
* *Judgment to ACCEPTANCE*
* *Problem to OPPORTUNITY*
* *Risk to ADVENTURE*
* *Attachment to DEDICATION*

* *Regret to AWARENESS*
* *Hurt to UNDERSTANDING*
* *Breakdown to BREAKTHROUGH*

It doesn't have to be an opposite; it can be a slight enough variation that it becomes a healthier and more centered emotion or state of being. For example, you don't have to jump from unmotivated to motivated, you can flip the switch to "interested" to start with. Then when you've embraced that, you can flip again to "inspired," "motivated," or "enthusiastic," making it an easier and more gradual progression.

ACTIVITY

There are two main ways to incorporate this practice into your life this week:

1. Be aware of what you're feeling, decide what you want to feel instead (or what feels achievable or slightly better at this point), and flip the switch. To flip, you can simply tell yourself that you are choosing to feel this way instead, or think thoughts that better serve the emotion you want. Or, you can go to a light switch and physically flip the switch while stating what you're flipping to. For example, if you've had a tough day and you're about to go to bed, when you turn off the light, turn off the negative emotion with it, flipping it to what you want. Before you turn off the switch, say, "I am turning off overwhelmed and turning on calm." Flip the switch, take a breath, and consciously embrace the feeling of calm (or whichever emotion you're wanting). If there is no switch around, you can even just pretend you're flipping a switch and press your finger against something to symbolize it. Try it now. Tune in to any emotion that is not exactly what you want to experience and flip a switch to what you *do* want.

2. Choose one to three emotional states that are common or recurring for you, and decide what you'll flip them to. Throughout the week look for those new emotions or states of being in the world around you, and make an effort to embrace those states yourself. For example, look for examples of dedication or understanding, then act with dedication yourself, and seek to understand a different perspective or understand more about yourself. Write below or in your journal the emotions/states you are choosing and what you're going to flip them to. You don't have to stick to the list in this chapter. You can choose your own.

_____

_____

_____

_____

_____

_____

_____

_____

_____

_____

11

A DIFFERENT APPROACH

When you take a different approach with something you'd normally do a certain way, it helps rewire your brain and develop new synapses (the junctions between nerve cells where chemicals transmit signals or instructions to perform a certain function). The more we challenge ourselves in new ways, the more adaptable our brains can become. This is helpful for coping with stress and change, and supporting our mental and neurological health. When you consciously give your brain a chance to adapt to new experiences without the stress that unexpected or sudden changes may cause, it helps your brain to learn that change doesn't have to be stressful for the nervous system.

Think about some tasks in your life that you could do a different way:

✳ *Drive a different route to work, or to the supermarket.*

✳ *Order something different from a menu or cook something different instead of your usual meals.*

✳ *Do certain tasks in a different order.*

✳ *Comment positively on a few social media posts that you would normally either just click "like" on or scroll past.*

✳ *Avoid commenting on certain posts of a negative nature that you would normally want to comment on, so that you don't add energy to the issue.*

✳ *Change your bedtime routine. For example, if you normally use your phone in bed, put it in a different room one night and go to bed with a book or a journal and pen, or do some mindful coloring, with no distractions.*

✳ *Wear something different. If you're a jeans person, try a skirt or dress, or a different type of trousers, or vice versa. If you wear a lot of dark or neutral colors, wear something bright.*

What else could you do differently? Have some fun with it.

ACTIVITY

It's time to try writing and drawing with your nondominant hand! This allows you to bypass your mind's judgment on what it should look like and allows your inner child and intuition to come through. (If you have a disability that means you only have use of one hand or have limited function, you may adapt this exercise however you wish, or try holding the pencil between different fingers).

Using your journal or the space on the facing page, do the following with your nondominant hand:

✻ *Draw yourself as a child.*

✻ *Draw yourself as an adult.*

✻ *Draw three of your favorite things (flowers, cake, books, trees, cats, etc.).*

✻ *Set a timer for one minute and draw freehand a pattern or scene with your nondominant hand without lifting your pencil or pen. You could try doing this each night this week.*

✻ *Write your answers to the following prompts (you can use your dominant hand for this!):*

• *If I could do anything I would . . .*

• *I feel like myself when I . . .*

• *What my soul needs most right now is . . .*

Don't judge your answers. They don't even have to be realistic. Just write the first thought that comes to mind.

Let's get your brain used to adapting!

MY DRAWING SPACE

12

FEEL-GOOD PLAYLIST

Music is a wonderful way to help you with your emotions and to shift your vibration. It is well-documented how certain types of music (and sound waves in general) can have an impact on your brain and heart, and even inflammation in the body. It can help you boost mood, relax, energize, and connect. It can also help you re-center.

Think back to some memories you have where music played a part.

* *A wedding*
* *A birthday*
* *A movie theme song on your first date*
* *Singing to your child*
* *Fun times with friends*
* *Your first music concert*
* *Your favorite TV show theme song*
* *Hearing a song on the radio that brings back memories and moves you to tears*

There's no doubt that music has the power to instantly impact our state of mind. Use this to your advantage on your centering journey.

ACTIVITY

Close your eyes and take some deep breaths. What type of music or which song makes you feel centered in some way? See if anything comes to mind. It may make you feel calm, or enthusiastic, at peace, or excited. It may just speak to your heart or make you feel like *you*. Jot it down, then repeat the process. What else comes to mind? If you have trouble thinking of more, go on YouTube and search for the first piece of music you chose and see what else comes up as suggested.

This week, create a feel-good playlist of at least five songs or pieces of music to listen to whenever you want to feel happy, calm, and centered. Play this as often as possible during the week. You might like to listen while getting ready for work, doing housework, taking a bath, or out for a walk. Feeling uncentered? Listen to your playlist and shift those vibrations back to center. Let yourself enjoy the healing sounds of music.

> **PS:** While I was writing this chapter, I had the TV on in the background. A song played in an ad and instantly I was transported to my teenage years. It's magical how it makes you feel.

13

THE CONTINUUM

See your day-to-day life and time as a continuum; a continual flow of never-ending energy that forms itself into pockets of time or opportunities, rather than a day with a beginning and an end, and then another separate day and so on. This can help avoid dissatisfaction and feelings of being overwhelmed when you feel like you can't get it all done each day.

It can be helpful to use the cycles of day and night to schedule our lives but it can also be helpful to see things as an overall continuum where nothing is ever behind or late, it's simply not yet at the present point along the continuum.

Each thing you do or want to do or need to do will come to the present point at some stage, but allow yourself to be where you are now on the continuum and know that you can't jump ahead or force its flow, you can only flow with it.

If you haven't achieved all you hoped to in a day, and you get to bed frustrated or feeling like things are unfinished, just see bedtime and sleep as another notch on the continuum that is moving you forward, and the flow will continue when you wake up.

Try planning your schedule with more flow and flexibility, and don't try to squeeze so many things into one day. You might choose to do certain things every second day, or three times a week instead of daily, or you might schedule your week's activities over a fortnight instead to spread some things out and feel like there is more time. It is what we do consistently over a longer period of time that matters most, so don't worry if every day doesn't pan out exactly as planned or hoped. For example, you don't have to use social media daily or respond to messages daily if you don't want to or need to. You could use it every second day and still get the same benefit, while giving you more time for other things on the alternate day.

Apart from time planning, which is still needed in order to function in society, when it comes to your perception of time, just remember the continuum, like a stream of flowing water, as that will give you more peace of mind and a greater sense of freedom, and help you to stay more in your center.

You can use a continuum timeline for both acknowledgment of your progress and for planning your activities or goals. To do this, simply draw a horizontal line in the middle of a piece of paper from left to right, or in your journal (the latter allows you to continue the line on subsequent pages). Every so often add a little notch and write the progress you made or an activity you accomplished, then start a new page when the first is full.

Or, add a notch and write tasks you want to complete, in order of priority or importance so that you can see this as a variation of a To Do list and/or daily timetable, but without the time constraints. It's simply a visual way to see your upcoming activities without the added pressure of a timeframe next to it—as the continuum is always flowing, you know you will reach each notch eventually at the right time. If things need to change order or direction as life unfolds, just as water may flow in a different direction to bypass an obstacle, simply cross them out and move them to a different notch. Keep the continuum fluid and flexible. Then, unlike a daily schedule or calendar where you turn the page and the day is gone along with various incomplete tasks, the continuum stays put. No matter what day it is you can write an activity on it once and keep it there, ready to cross off whenever it is done.

Try this with tasks that don't require a specific deadline and see how it feels. Does it take the pressure off? By mapping your progress in this way you can see what you have accomplished and know that because the continuum is always flowing you will reach more notches and accomplish more as you move along with the flow without forcing it or trying to jump ahead too quickly.

ACTIVITY

Try creating a continuum line in your journal, adding tasks in order of priority as notches along the flow of time, but without adding a day or time to them. You can do an overall continuum or separate continuum lines for different goals or projects, breaking down each one into different milestones to reach or complete. Or, create a continuum line where you add milestones or tasks as they are completed, to see how you are progressing and give you confidence that you are moving forward.

Also try saying this affirmation to help you stay centered during busy times or those days when you feel behind with everything:

> *"I flow with the continuum of life and trust that everything happens at the right time for me."*

14

SACRED SPACES

Create a sacred space, or spaces, in your environment—areas that are clear of clutter, feel special, and that only contain objects you want to be there.

First, tune in to the sacred space within yourself, like a portal to your center, and then create extensions of that in physical form. Use your inner sacred space as a gateway to your center, a home for your center, supporting and nourishing it. Visualize a space that looks and feels special and sacred to you. It might be a beautiful garden or a vast landscape or high up in a treehouse or even outer space. Sort of like your happy place, your sacred space is an aspect of this, something you can imagine when you need to feel comforted and safe. Then from this space you can more easily access your center, like finding your favorite comfy chair (your center) in your house (sacred space).

You can also visualize a sacred space within certain parts of your body, such as your heart, an area of discomfort or dis-ease, or for females, your womb, as a way to embody love and well-being in this area and honor its sacredness. This can be a powerful form of self-healing, drawing nourishing thoughts and energy to areas in the body that need it.

Now, find an area in your home or work environment to create a physical representation of your sacred space, such as a room that's just for you and everything that makes you feel centered. It could be a shelf, a cupboard, a wall, a part of a garden, a tree, or a garage. Make it so that every time you visit, you feel at home and centered. Even if you have a lot of clutter around you, are sharing space with others, have messy family members, or you're moving house or unpacking or renovating, find at least one small space that you can make into a sacred space. It can even just be a bedside table or the top of a bookcase or a windowsill. Make as many sacred spaces as you like. Look at this space or these spaces when you want to feel more connected to your center.

ACTIVITY

When you've decided on your sacred space, add whatever you like to your space to help it feel sacred and special. It could be a single candle, a feather, a crystal or collection of crystals, a statue or symbol, a bowl of rose petals, a small vase or bud vase and a fresh flower or posy, a framed print or quote, or a few of your favorite inspirational books. Choose what you place there purposefully so that it has meaning and significance for you.

You can use this space as a reminder to practice mindfulness or centering strategies. You can also use it as a space you visit and focus on when you want to set intentions, pray, or talk to your loved ones in spirit, or your spiritual guides when you need assistance.

Most of all, when you see this space, remind yourself that you also have a sacred space *within* you that is always available to you, and the more you connect with it consciously, the more peaceful your experience of life becomes.

You may even wish to share a photo of your sacred space online to inspire others. Use the hashtag #returntocenterbook and #sacredspace.

15

WHAT WOULD IT TAKE?

What would it take for you to be living a life you love? What would it take for you to feel centered more often?

Think about it: what would it *actually* take? A change in circumstances like a new job or home, an increase in income, or simply a change in perspective?

List in your journal as many things as you can that come to mind, things that would help you live the life that you want, whether you know how to get them or not. For example: to get more sleep, to have a more supportive or understanding partner, to have more money, to spend more time doing things you love, to find your soulmate, to be free of pain, to meditate more, to be grateful for what you have, to have less housework to do, to win the lottery, to learn a new skill, to find supportive and like-minded friends, etc.

If it helps, start with the sentence: "To live the life I want, it would take. . ." or, "To live the life I want, I feel I would need. . ."

When you've written a list, get two pieces of paper (or use your journal, although you'll be tearing out one page after), and on the first one write the heading:

THINGS I CAN CONTROL

On the second page write the heading:

THINGS FOR THE UNIVERSE TO HANDLE (or God, Spirit, etc.)

On the first page, write those things from your list that you CAN control (at least to a certain degree), and on the second page write things outside of your direct control. Some things may fit on both, in which case add them to both; or add an extra bit of information to specify what it is you can control and what you can't. For example, if you feel you would need a pay raise, what is in your control is "asking for a pay raise" or "doing an exceptional job at work," and what is under the universe's control is, "my boss choosing to give me a pay raise or promotion." In that case, you break down the item into an aspect you can act on while surrendering the other aspect to the universe and taking the pressure off yourself.

ACTIVITY

Make an effort this week to do something from the first page (things you can control), and put the other page into an envelope or a small box just for the universe, God, your spirit guides, spirit, source energy, guardian angels, or whichever spiritual energy you identify with most and believe can help you.

Ask them to help with these things out of your control and then drop the page into the box or fold it into the envelope, and then let those things go. Surrender your attachment to outcomes. Take back your power and focus on what you can actually do. Those other things are no longer weighing you down, no longer in your job description. Focus on the first list of things you can control, and when you feel life getting in your way or holding you back, return to this list and know that you have power to change certain things and that worrying about what you can't control is a waste of your precious emotional energy.

It's important to point out that "out of your control" doesn't necessarily mean you can't have an impact on it. You still can, but only by changing your own perspectives or actions that can then create a shift in vibration. This allows a stream of energy and focus toward the direction you would like things to go, and the law of attraction can follow and help orchestrate the other things that will help you live the life you want.

You can also add future things separately to the envelope or box as needed. Such as getting the job you want or recovering from your health condition. Simply say, "Universe, please help me with the issue of [state the issue]." Then put the piece of paper with the issue written on it inside the envelope. Once you create your lists and put the second page away, you should feel empowered and relieved.

16

MORNING Ms

Each morning when you wake, before you roll over and grab your phone, before you jump out of bed to get dressed, or make breakfast, or talk to anyone, take some time just for yourself for your "Morning Ms," or "MMM":

Mindfulness

Mantra

Movement

MINDFULNESS

Become aware that you're now awake and present in your room. Notice how your body feels against the bed, how it supports you, the curves and bumps in contact with your body. Feel the temperature of your body and the air around you. Are there areas of warmth and areas of coolness? Breathe in deeply and feel the air passing through your nostrils. Listen for sounds around you, and outside. Are there any scents in the air? Notice something in your surroundings and focus on it: your bedside lamp, a book, a candle, or a corner of the wall. Simply notice, and be aware, without thinking deeply. This mindfulness helps anchor you in the present moment and transition you from dream life to daily life.

If you feel like it and you have time, you can extend this practice to another M: meditation. Simply focus on your breathing and imagine your mind is a clear blue sky, any thoughts passing by as gentle clouds that simply float away when you notice them, restoring your blue sky mind.

MANTRA:

After your mindfulness and/or meditation, choose a short statement or intention for the day, or just for the moment; a mantra to guide and support you.

Examples:

I am calm and at ease.

All is well.

Today is a wonderful gift.
I am showered with blessings today.
I love my life.
I feel well and happy today.

Or anything that feels good to you.
Say it three times out loud or in your mind, and smile.

MOVEMENT

Either move in bed before getting up, or get out of bed and move your body in a comfortable, nourishing way. You could hug your knees to your chest and then roll them to one side, stretching your hips. You could roll your head from side to side while being supported by the pillow to ease any tension. You could stand up on your toes and stretch your arms up high. You could bend forward and hang your head upside down for a while. You could jiggle or sway, or do any of the movements from the Move Your Energy chapter.

If you like, repeat your mantra at the end of your movements, then go about your day.

The more you practice this and remind yourself, the more automatic it becomes. It will be a normal and automatic start to your day, helping you begin with a clean slate.

ACTIVITY

Do your Morning Ms every day this week. Continue beyond that time if you like. You can also repeat the process throughout the day as needed to re-center, as a transition from one task to the next. You can also do night Ms if you wish, but in reverse, with the movement being first and being different—more of a calming and grounding movement to relax you and prepare for sleep.

Each morning, remind yourself, "Time to do my Morning Ms! Mmm!"

17

REFRAME

We have so many thoughts going around in our minds at any given moment. Some we are extremely aware of, and some are so fleeting we barely notice them. Others are recurring and have been for a long time, so we tend to think of them as just part of us, just the way we are. But they are not part of us; we are *not* our thoughts. With a bit of conscious effort, we can become more aware of those recurring thoughts that are not helping us and take steps to change them, by reframing.

Conscious reframing is when you notice a thought about something and you realize it's not really in your best interests, so you change it slightly, or even dramatically, to a new thought that better serves you but is still true. Often, we are reluctant to change our thoughts because we either believe we can't help it (and that belief itself is just another recurring thought), or we have a need to be right and to explain what is going on to validate what we're experiencing. But all you are really explaining is what has been true up to that moment. And you can either let history keep repeating itself or you can take action to change it.

The more you consciously choose a new thought, the easier it gets to keep thinking that new thought, until eventually it becomes automatic and recurring, just like the previous thought. Many unhelpful thoughts were instilled in our minds from a young age when we didn't have the awareness or maturity to change them. It is up to us *now* to take that step and help that younger part of us out, by reframing, so that we can establish new and more helpful thought patterns.

When you find yourself thinking recurring negative thoughts, stop for a moment and ask yourself, "Is that really true? And then, what else could be true? What is another way of thinking about this? Or, what about this do I want to be true?"

The best way to explain reframing is through examples, so read through the following and acknowledge any that feel true for you, and see if you can think of others unique to your situation.

"I never have enough time for what I want to do!"

Reframe: "Up until now I haven't had enough time for what I want to do, but from now on I'm going to make time."

Or: "I have the same amount of time as everyone else and I deserve to spend a good chunk of it doing things I love."

See how the above is still a true thought but from a different perspective? It's one that is helpful and filled with hope rather than one that is limiting.

"No one ever listens to me."

Reframe: "I listen to myself and respond to my own needs."

"I'm always late!"

Reframe: "I've often been late before, but I'm in the process of learning to better manage my time."

"Bad things just keep happening!"

Reframe: "There is always something good in my life, and I choose to focus on the good things more than the bad things."

Or: "Good things keep happening too!"

"I can't afford it."

Reframe: "It's not a priority in my budget right now."

Or: "This is important to me and I'll save for it."

"My husband/wife is so annoying sometimes!"

Reframe: "I have a husband/wife who loves me and I love him/her. I'm so grateful."

"It's too cold in my house!"

Reframe: "I'm so grateful to have a roof over my head."

"My stomach/thighs/ankles are too fat."

Reframe: "I have a living, breathing body. What a gift to be alive!"

ACTIVITY

Do any of those resonate with you? Are there any other negative thoughts or complaints you often find yourself thinking? Write them down and then create a reframe.

You can actually change your life, one thought at a time.

_____

_____

_____

_____

_____

_____

_____

_____

_____

_____

_____

_____

_____

_____

_____

_____

18

PULL BACK

This lesson is about the energy that stems from your center and radiates out to the world around you and toward whatever you are focusing your attention on. Where your attention goes, energy flows, so you want to make sure your precious energy from the core of your being is going where it is wanted, and not being spread too far and wide.

Every time you look closely at something, read an article, watch a video, or observe something around you, that is your center energy being directed. Are you directing it at something worthy?

Whenever you are about to get drawn into something, I want you to ask yourself, "Is this where I want my energy to flow?"

If not, pull back. And by this, I mean consciously imagining your energy being drawn back into yourself. Like a vacuum sucking in air, but a bit gentler. Try bringing your energy back with each inhalation to give that power and focus back to yourself. Visualize the streams of energy you've radiated outward flowing back to you, your center, your core, to nourish and stabilize your energy. Fill yourself up with this loving energy before spreading it outward again.

If there is something you must focus on even if you don't want to, or if it makes you upset or uncomfortable, visualize one thin stream of energy going to that issue, but the rest curling back into yourself. This way, an aspect of you and your energy can be there in real life, assisting someone or dealing with something challenging but necessary, and at the same time you can remain strong and grounded in your center.

ACTIVITY

Try practicing this with your breath. Notice the world around you and feel your energy going outward, then consciously pull it back toward you and within you. Feel your center getting stronger. You always have this power. You don't have to let external circumstances take your energy or power away.

When you notice yourself feeling affected by external circumstances, mentally say, "Pull back," then practice this technique. It might be a heated discussion on Facebook, an argument, gossip, something negative in the media, or even just too much stimulation, and the noise of life in general.

Pull your energy back and reclaim your power.

19

APPRECIATE

You've heard of gratitude lists and gratitude journals, but something even more powerful for raising your vibration and aligning yourself with your center is an Appreciation List.

When you genuinely appreciate something you are tuned in to your core, and you are not in a state of neediness, but of calm satisfaction and peace. Gratitude is also powerful, but sometimes holds an additional vibration of struggle because it is often associated with the opposite of something unpleasant. For example, you can be grateful for your blood pressure being back to normal after working on it, and this is great, but it also hints at it having been "not normal" at some stage, associating your gratitude with something having been out of sorts or off-center.

Appreciation is like a step up from gratitude. Start with gratitude if it's easier, because gratitude is still very powerful, but then step up to appreciation, which has a softer vibration that helps release resistance and allow your alignment. For example, "I appreciate the amazing work my heart does every day keeping me healthy," as opposed to, "I'm grateful my blood pressure is back to normal." See the difference?

An appreciation practice can involve big things or little things. It can include things like: "I appreciate how Mother Earth supports me and provides for me," or simply, "I appreciate the beautiful pattern on that leaf."

Get into an appreciation practice every day this week if you can, in the morning or before bed.

ACTIVITY

Set a timer for 4 minutes and write down as many things as possible that you appreciate right now in your life, whether highly significant or simple. This could include having a support network, the freedom to express yourself on social media, the pretty pattern on your cushion, the genuine smile from a sales assistant, the comforting taste of your daily tea, etc.

How many things did you list in 4 minutes? If you do this daily, don't be surprised if you have an extra-amazing week with lots to appreciate.

PS: I appreciate you reading this book!

_____

_____

_____

_____

_____

_____

_____

_____

_____

20

WANTING & GIVING

What do you want, right now? Say it. Out loud. Not what you want next week or next year or in five years' time, but right now. In this very moment.

Do you want peace and quiet, a nap, or a nice hot chocolate? Or perhaps you want affection, even a simple hug.

Say it, no matter what it is. If people are around you and it's not appropriate to speak it out loud, say it in your mind and then reaffirm it out loud when you can. Feel the liberation of declaring what you actually want.

If what you want is something you can easily experience right now, and it is genuinely healthy for your mind, body, heart, or spirit, and not an addiction, then go experience it.

Enjoy it. Acknowledge and satisfy your desires. If it's not something you can get immediately, then take a step of some kind toward it.

If you can't easily get what it is you want, then GIVE it, in some form or another, literally or metaphorically, to yourself or someone else. This should be done in a consenting way, of course, depending on what it is. What is the perceived benefit of what you want? How can you give that to yourself and/or another person? For example, the benefit of affection may be connection, or comfort. How can you connect with and comfort yourself, or another person? The easiest way to get what you want is to give it first—not in a greedy way with an agenda, but with a kind heart, knowing that you actually do have that "thing" to give. This makes it feel not so difficult to get it for yourself also, because in some form you already have it.

If you want a hug and no one is around, hug yourself. Hug an animal. If loved ones are around, ask who would like a hug, and tell them you appreciate them. Find how you can experience, give, or embrace what it is you're wanting, even if it's just stating it out loud and then letting go and allowing the universe to work its magic.

Examples:

❋ *I want some company – go ahead and provide companionship to someone else who needs it, perhaps someone who needs it even more than you do.*

❋ *I want more money – give some away. I know it sounds counterintuitive, but the act of giving shows that you are abundant, and the universe matches this vibration with more abundance. I once donated $50 to a charity, not because someone knocked on my door or sent me a letter or approached me in a shopping mall, but because I genuinely wanted to give to this particular cause. A week later, I won $50 on a $2 lottery ticket. The universe always rewards a pure vibration of kindness in some way.*

❋ *I want more rest – have a nap, and/or ask someone in need (like a tired parent) if they'd like you to watch their child while they get some rest.*

ACTIVITY

List a few things (here or in your journal) that you are wanting, and next to each write down how you can give this to yourself or another person, either directly, or the perceived benefit of it.

_____

_____

_____

_____

_____

21

QUOTE IT

Sometimes feeling off-center is the result of an inner need to feel heard or understood. First, always seek to hear and understand yourself, and hear and understand others, before seeking external validation or acknowledgment. Always look at how you can give to yourself more.

Apart from a need to feel heard and understood, become aware of what your core *off-center* feelings actually are (loneliness, frustration, being misunderstood, feeling overstimulated and overwhelmed, feeling like the odd one out or lacking a sense of belonging, etc.). Then look up quotes that relate to those feelings; for example, by typing "quotes on understanding" or "quotes on feeling lonely" into a search engine or Pinterest (picture quotes are usually easier to browse through). Find and save those that resonate with you—the ones that make you say, "Yes! That's exactly how I feel."

Sometimes just doing that for yourself is enough to feel heard, to know that someone else out there gets it. If you like, you could post one of the quotes on your social media to spread awareness of that particular issue or emotion, and you may even find other people responding in agreement. Then you are helping other people to feel heard and understood too, while also helping yourself. You may even find that the issue you were struggling with becomes eased by reaching out and connecting with others, who may either resonate with you, or offer support.

ACTIVITY

Think about what your feelings are when you are off-center, or anything you are feeling or struggling with right now. Find quotes relating to those feelings and save them somewhere you can easily access them in the future—an image folder on your phone or computer, a Pinterest quote board, printed out and pasted on cardboard or in a journal, or written out into a quote journal. If you feel like sharing, share one online—you might just help someone else. Feel free to write one right here.

22

ANIMAL INSTINCT

There's something about animals that brings you back to the simplicity of life. They have a way of both distracting you and focusing you, helping you be in a more centered state. Often when I've felt overwhelmed or out of sorts, I've spent some time with my cats—stroking their fur, playing, watching—and it brings me back to the moment. It helps refresh and restore, shifting negative vibrations. Connecting with animals can help reduce stress, boost mood, and enhance feelings of connection and companionship.

Take some time this week to connect with an animal. If you don't have any animals around you, find a way to spend time with one soon, perhaps with a friend's pet, at an animal shelter, or at a zoo. Or visit a park and watch the birdlife. Or even just look at cute and funny animal photos and videos online, or watch an animal documentary. Enjoy the simple pleasure of being in an animal's presence. Remember, if it's helping you to return to center, it's not a waste of time.

Animals can also help to remind us to not overthink, and to follow our natural instincts. Animals don't create detailed plans or have high expectations, they just live in the moment and follow their instincts. They get on with things as best they can with what they have.

Of course, as humans we do have to make plans and think ahead, but we often go overboard with these things at the expense of accepting the gift of each moment.

ACTIVITY

Make a list of animals that you love in particular. Spend some time with those you have access to, and observe how they live in the moment.

Focus on going with the flow of your natural instincts this week as much as possible. And if you feel off-center at any time, look at an animal photo or video and let it soothe and comfort you and bring a smile to your face. When you smile, your center does too.

_____

_____

_____

_____

_____

_____

_____

_____

_____

_____

23

RITUALS

A ritual is any process or action that is done with intention and mindfulness, and often associated with a particular event, experience, or purpose, as a one-off or repeated process. Rituals are a powerful way to focus and direct your energy, and they help you come from your center.

Create a ritual that you do on a daily or weekly basis to act as a centering, grounding process to connect you with your divine power and your calm, pure essence. Rituals give us a sense of peaceful and joyous anticipation and a sense of inner stability and control in our lives. Like a daily meditation practice, a ritual gives us something to look forward to and something to give us familiarity and comfort, knowing that whatever happens in our day, we have the reassurance of our ritual to keep us feeling tuned in and balanced.

Through ritual you can more fully embrace and embody the spiritual (spiRITUAL).

Many of the activities in this book are rituals themselves, and you can incorporate some of them more regularly and intentionally into your life; however, you can also create your own. Think of rituals as a step-by-step process that you associate with a part of your life. Like a choreography, a dance, a harmonious sequence of steps that merge together to create something meaningful.

Ritual ideas:

✻ *Create a Sunday night or Monday morning 5-minute intention ritual for the week ahead when you consciously decide what to embody or create. For example, "This week I am committed to bringing joy to every situation I encounter." Or, "This week I am following my body's cues and putting myself first." Whatever feels right to you.*

✻ *Have an end of the week self-love bath, with bath salts, essential oils, candles, and music or silence, and finish it off with a slow and mindful self-massage with luxurious body lotion.*

✻ *As a daily ritual, do your Morning Ms (from chapter 16).*

✻ *For another daily ritual, every time you wash your hands throughout the day, do it for a good twenty seconds and completely immerse yourself in appreciation for the sensations—the coolness or warmth of the water, the light pressure of the water flow, the feeling of being cleansed and refreshed, the amazing gift that water is to our lives. Be mindful and grateful and look forward to this mini-mindfulness moment throughout each day.*

✻ *On every full moon, have a release ritual. State out loud or write down what you wish to let go of in your life. If you've written it down, tear the paper up afterward or burn it. It might be an attachment to a past relationship, a negative self-talk habit, unhealthy eating patterns, etc.*

✻ *On every new moon, have a manifestation ritual. State out loud or write down what you wish to bring into your life. It might be a new relationship, a positive body image, healthy eating patterns, an increase in income, a new job opportunity, anything that you desire. You might wish to "program" a specific crystal with your intentions and keep it close by throughout the month.*

ACTIVITY

What rituals feel good to you? Write down the daily and/or weekly ritual or rituals you'd like to incorporate into your life here or in your journal, and outline the steps involved in each. Schedule these rituals into your calendar.

Daily Rituals:

_____

_____

_____

_____

Weekly Rituals:

_____

_____

_____

_____

24

FIND YOUR RHYTHM

It's easier to return to center and stay centered when you allow yourself to follow your natural rhythm. By this I mean listening to your body's timing and following your internal clock. This is not always possible in modern life, when the clock runs our day and we have to be "on time" to things, but whenever you have the chance, take time off, literally. Take time off from time. Whether it's for just part of your day, a whole day, or a few days, commit to either eliminating or reducing your reliance on the clock. It can be challenging to find space to actually do this and then to follow through with it, but once you try it, you'll feel the benefits and the sense of freedom that comes with it.

Take off your watch, take the clocks down off the wall, and unplug digital clocks. Turn off phone reminder apps, or even your phone. Spend some time following your natural rhythms and listening to your body and soul. Live in moments, not minutes.

If you do have a day or an afternoon off, try not checking the time or technology at all and just let your body decide when it's time for things such as eating, resting, and activity. The outside world will let you know when it's getting late, your body will tell you when it's hungry, and your soul will tell you what's important in each moment.

If you can have a regular "time-free" afternoon or day off every now and again, it will allow your body to naturally center itself, and you'll be more aware during your on-the-clock days of what you need at certain times and when to do things. You'll find more of a natural rhythm within yourself that will benefit your daily life and find that you don't need to check what time it is as often.

Time pressure is a common stress for many people, so training yourself not to be so reliant on it, and instead trusting that your body knows when to do certain things (except if you're at work and have responsibilities affecting others), can take a lot of that stress away.

ACTIVITY

1. Are you prepared to take the time-free challenge and find your rhythm? Choose an afternoon, a day, or a segment of your life when you don't have anything urgent or time-sensitive later on, when you can switch off your time-related technology for a while and listen to your body's cues, and those of nature. Every time you get an urge to check the time or look at your phone, remind yourself to just breathe and be in the moment.

2. Discover your personal, natural rhythm by working out what times of the day or night you do certain things better, in terms of being more efficient or happier doing certain tasks. When do you find it easiest to be logical, creative, productive, and communicative or social? Depending on your job or responsibilities, try to put tasks relating to these areas in the time segment that best allows you to complete them more effortlessly and naturally. For example, you might find you're better at logical and communicative tasks in the morning before lunch, so this is the most natural time for you to schedule those sorts of tasks. You might find your creativity peaks in the evening or late at night, so perhaps that is the best time for creative pursuits—or you might find those pursuits are better accomplished first thing in the morning. Try a few different times and see when feels best, to find your natural rhythm.

25

ASK YOUR GUIDES

To help you gain support in returning to center and finding clarity and confidence in your next steps, asking your guides can help.

Who are your guides? I'm talking about spirit guides—your spiritual support team, who are always there for you in the spiritual or energetic realm. We all have spiritual assistance guiding us through life.

You don't have to know much about spirituality or intuitive communication to ask your spirit guides for help. You can do this simply by believing, then asking verbally or writing to them. You can ask for their help in small matters or big matters. Nothing is too much or too little for them.

Most of us have several spirit guides, who may be those who've passed over, and/or those who have not been in physical form but are divine beings of energy and focused consciousness. If you find it hard to grasp, just remember everything is energy, including us, and energy never dies. You can communicate with your guides as often or as little as you wish, but they are always standing by to help, a bit like guardian angels.

When I need assistance, sometimes I ask the universe, or God, or I'll simply ask my spirit guides as it feels more personal. I might say out loud something like, "Dear Guides, I'd love you to reserve a parking spot for me right near the café today." (Sounds silly but it's amazing how often it actually works.)

Or it might be more significant, like, "Dear Guides, I'm really struggling today, please show me the way to feeling better."

They love it when you're direct and specific, as they can help more appropriately.

If you don't want to ask out loud, or want to try a different method, writing a letter to your guides for assistance is a great way to communicate with them, and often to get answers back, too.

You could write whenever you need help, or you can make it a regular letter each week or each day. Start small with just a short statement or question and build up until you get used to communicating with them.

Write about how you're feeling and tell them how you'd like to feel, and then what you'd like help with. You could release each letter gratefully or keep them in a "Dear Guides" journal.

Sometimes I've written two or three pages detailing everything that's weighing on my mind and all the things I need help with. The writing process itself is a great release, but it's more than that, because if you write with genuine intent and belief, I guarantee they will hear, and they will get to work on your behalf. You can surrender and trust.

ACTIVITY

Practice asking your guides out loud for help, and try writing a letter with one or two things you'd like assistance with, or a letter detailing everything currently on your mind that you'd like to feel better about. Then follow your intuitive nudges, take opportunities, and do what feels right, as their support may come in unexpected ways.

_____

_____

_____

_____

_____

26

LET GO

W e are often so focused on what we need to do, have, or experience to regain our balance and center, that something just as powerful can be forgotten: what we need to *let go* of.

By letting go of what is no longer serving us, we let in what does.

By releasing what doesn't matter, we regain what does.

Letting go creates a vacuum effect and space for the law of attraction to fill.

Is there something you need to let go of? It could be emotional or physical. Perhaps something in your schedule or To Do list, an object in your house that doesn't resonate with you, ties to an old relationship or friendship that no longer serves you, or an unhealthy eating habit. It could also be an over-attachment to the past, whether it's the past from long ago or simply the past week.

Decide on one or two things you will take action on this week to release or let go of. It might be a complete release, or one step toward a more gradual release.

You can let go by simply declaring your intention, physically getting rid of something, writing a letter, blocking certain people or pages on social media, avoiding commenting on negative posts, having a full-moon releasing ritual, having an energy healing, changing your habits, or removing something unnecessary from your schedule.

There is a lightness and re-centering that comes from letting go. And by surrendering, ironically you also gain more of a sense of control over your life, because the act of letting go declares to the universe that you won't stand for anything that's not in alignment with your highest good or true self.

Here are some ideas of things to work on releasing in your life.

* *Limiting beliefs*
* *Past relationships*
* *Unhealthy connections*
* *Clutter – physical*
* *Old sentimental objects that no longer benefit you*
* *Clutter – digital*
* *Expectations*
* *Resentments*
* *Perfection*
* *Past hurts*
* *Attachment to outcome*
* *Fear*
* *Regrets*
* *Judgment*
* *Negative self-talk*
* *The need to apologize*
* *Worry*
* *Unhealthy habits*
* *Situations you can't control*

ACTIVITY

What do you choose to let go of?

Write down the following and fill in the blanks for each thing you'd like to release:

"I choose to let go of [this] now, because [reason why it's holding you back], and I look forward to freeing up space to allow [what you'd like to let in].
I will release this by [how you will let go of it]."

Then follow through with a release in whatever form you decide.

_____

_____

_____

_____

_____

_____

_____

_____

27

CRYSTALLIZE

Crystals are a great way to help you return to center, because they themselves are like a center: a concentrated, high vibration focal point of pure positive energy.

Crystals can help in two ways: unconsciously, by their subtle but direct influence on energy, and consciously, by your attention to them alongside your intentions. Crystals are a gift from Mother Nature that help you tune in to your own true nature, and all the infinite resources that reside there within.

You can choose a crystal that embodies the energy you want to embrace, or you can choose a crystal you just like the look of or feel drawn to and make it your intention crystal or your centering crystal.

When you need help returning to center, hold your crystal and say, "Return to center," or any of your preferred affirmations that help you tune in to your happy place.

If you have crystals at home, choose one to be your centering crystal, or choose a crystal for the day or the week ahead and program it with your intention or chosen affirmation. If you don't own any crystals, find a crystal store, or a supplier online, and choose one you feel connected to.

First, return to center with it by sitting quietly and holding it in your hands. Breathe and feel it becoming warmer, try to tune in to the subtle but strong vibrations it holds within. What is it trying to tell you? See the crystal as a conduit to your soul, or your spirit guides, and ask for an insightful message to help you in this moment or during the coming week.

Next, decide what your main intention is for the day or week and program it into your crystal by holding it and looking at it while saying the intention out loud three times. For example, "I experience peaceful moments every day," or, "I radiate love and joy everywhere I go," or something more specific, like, "I see a rainbow this week as a sign from the universe that I'm on the right path."

Then close your eyes and hold it to your heart and say it three times silently within, feeling the crystal embodying that intention so that every time you look at or hold the crystal you will remember your intention. Carry it with you throughout the day and week.

You might like to write down any insights or messages that came to you while tuning in to your crystal.

Here are some crystals with calming, grounding, strengthening, uplifting, and revitalizing properties to help with returning to center:

* *Amethyst*
* *Red jasper*
* *Hematite*
* *Crazy lace agate*
* *Selenite*
* *Lepidolite*
* *Carnelian*

ACTIVITY

Choose your centering crystal, either one overall or one for the day or week ahead, and follow the steps above to program it and set your intention.

28

TRUST YOUR TRUTH

In a world with so much information at our fingertips, we can find out things we need to know in an instant. It's a wonderful thing, but when it comes to things we need to know about ourselves, our path, our future, and our truth, we can become conditioned to look externally for those things, too.

Constantly looking outside of ourselves can take us off-center.

There's nothing wrong with seeking guidance or advice from a professional or a psychic or from friends or family, but it's important to not lose connection to your own awareness and truth. External guidance can be very valuable and can also help you to feel less alone in certain situations. But take all the advice you receive on board and process it, then uncover your own inner truth from this and from your intuition.

Learn to trust yourself more. When you do, your inner guidance system and intuition will become stronger, giving you more recognizable clues to decipher your unique situation.

Don't let other people tell you what you should be feeling or doing. Trust your own emotional awareness and take actions aligned with your truth, and avoid taking action on those things that don't align with your truth.

I've received a lot of external advice, from both professionals and friends/family. Some I've agreed with, some I haven't. When I acted on the things that didn't feel totally right to me—things that made me feel off-center but I thought I should be doing anyway—it backfired and made things worse. So I decided to tune in and listen to what felt true to me deep inside. I acted on this, and things began shifting around me in better ways, bringing some much-needed relief and calm.

How do you know if the guidance or advice you're getting from someone is aligned with your truth?

By the way you feel.

Do you feel a closing off of your energy, or a confliction inside? Does it make you tense or uncertain?

It might not be your truth.

What feels better to you? What feels right for you? The best thing doesn't always have to feel comfortable, it could actually be something nerve-wracking or unpleasant, yet still feel *right*. It's when you feel an inner knowing that something is right and you feel an urge to act (or not act) in a certain way.

You can also tune in to your truth with some simple prompts. Try these in your journal, by thinking about a particular situation or just where you currently stand in your life journey:

MY TRUTH:

What I feel is. . .

What I know is. . .

What I want and deserve is. . .

What actions feel right (and not right) to me?

- An example scenario: let's say you are looking for a life partner. . .

What I feel is. . .
    disappointed, impatient, lonely, hopeful, excited (can be both positive and negative)

What I know is. . .
    there is someone out there for me
    I'm worthy of someone really special
    it could take time, but it could also happen tomorrow

What I want and deserve is. . .
    someone who shares my values
    someone who will make time for me
    to be treated with respect and understanding

What actions feel right (and not right) to me?

–Right:
Online dating
Going to events I'm passionate about
Dates in the outdoors doing healthy activities

–Not right:
Going to pubs
Being set up on blind dates
Drinking a lot of alcohol on dates
Meeting someone without talking on the phone first

By tuning in to these questions about particular aspects of your life, you can become aware of your truth first so that you're prepared for any advice-givers, and you'll more easily know when to take other suggestions or not. It'll also help you set boundaries around what you will and won't accept.

Be open to guidance, but always trust yourself first.

Trust your truth.

29

MAGIC MIRROR

Taking a good look at yourself, both physically and emotionally, can be equally confronting and liberating.

It is an act of self-love, to really see yourself, inside and outside.

To be seen, to be heard, to be accepted, to be understood, and to feel connected are common things we as humans crave, and yet many people seek to experience them outside of themselves. The most important thing you can do is give these things to yourself. When you do this, you're better able to do the same for others, and they're better able to do them for you.

See yourself, hear yourself, accept yourself, understand yourself, and connect with yourself. This helps you tune in to, embrace, and live from your center more fully.

To do this, use a real mirror first, and then a virtual mirror, to see what lies beneath the physical.

Right now if you can, find a mirror. The bigger the better. Look at as much of yourself as you can. And remember, you're only human. And not just only, but amazingly, magnificently, perfectly imperfectly human! Look at yourself and appreciate yourself for living life and doing your best. Give thanks for your eyes, ears, skin, smile, and any other body parts or features for the function they provide. Take a closer look at some of them. Marvel in the perfection of nature's design. Don't dwell on anything you haven't yet accepted about your physical self. Let yourself be human—forgive, accept, and appreciate yourself for who you are. And if you're ready, look yourself in the eyes and say, "I love you."

If you feel emotional during this process that's okay. It's a good thing. It means you're really seeing yourself and giving yourself the gift of this moment.

Give yourself a smile before turning away from the mirror.

ACTIVITY

After doing the physical mirror exercise on the previous page, complete the following virtual mirror exercise. Have a seat and imagine the palm of your nondominant hand is a mirror. Hold it in front of your body, somewhere around your heart area or solar plexus, anywhere you feel most connected to. Breathe deeply and tune in to your center. You might like to visualize it like we did in a previous chapter.

With your other hand, have a pen and notebook ready. Just like when you looked in the mirror and noticed various physical aspects of yourself and gave thanks for them, do the same for your inner aspects, your soul gifts, your center, by answering the following questions in your mind or writing them down:

1. Three qualities I admire most in myself are: (e.g., kindness, creativity, persistence)

2. My (first quality) has allowed me to. . . (help others, make someone smile, etc.). Answer this for each of the three qualities.

3. I forgive myself for. . . (state anything you feel you'd like to forgive yourself for: letting other people's views influence my decisions, not knowing how to trust myself, the mistakes I've made, etc.)

4. I'm proud of myself for. . . (committing to my self-care, sticking to my goals)

5. I love that my center is a place within I can always connect to that helps me feel. . . (calm, me, trusting, insightful)

6. I feel that my center contains the energy of the following colors:

7. The advice I have for myself today is:

Tuning in like this is a powerful way to connect to your center and to unite all aspects of yourself—physical, emotional, mental, and spiritual.

Hopefully you now have a greater appreciation and acceptance of yourself. Smile and know you've given yourself a wonderful gift. This is the magic of the mirror.

30

CENTERING SEQUENCE

Like yoga has a "salute to the sun" sequence, create your own physical movement sequence to symbolize returning to center. It could be a short series of yoga or tai chi postures/movements, a simple raising up and down of your arms three times, turning around on the spot, or a complex dance move.

Make it fun, easy, pleasing, and your own. I like to move my hands and arms up slowly in a flowing motion as I take a deep breath in, then push my palms down and outward when I exhale, as though pushing away any negativity. Then sometimes I'll do a spinal roll downward; tilting my head forward and letting my spine slowly roll down to hang my head upside down, and slowly roll up again, followed by a brief rise up and down on my toes.

It's not only good for your body, but having a centering sequence can help train your nervous system to relax and automatically trigger your return to center, and all the beneficial states of being it brings.

Whenever you feel off-center and if you're in an appropriate place, do your sequence to help re-center. Sometimes something physical like this is easier than thinking or feeling your way out of a slump. It's a good strategy when you feel stuck or have been overthinking.

Another movement-based option could include finding a door and walking through it purposefully, closing it behind you to symbolize leaving the past behind and stepping fully into your center.

What movements feel good to you? Your sequence can be anything you like and it doesn't have to be fancy or contain precise or performance-worthy movements. Work with your unique physical capabilities and don't do anything that puts a strain on you; it needs to be something easy and pleasurable to do. Try a few options and see what works. You could have a brief version and a longer version. Something you can easily do in a bathroom can be good too, for times when you're out and about or at work and need a private space to re-center.

ACTIVITY

Practice a few ideas for your centering sequence. You don't have to decide right away. It might take a few days of experimenting until you find something that feels right. If you need help, try putting on your favorite music, or watch a music video, or some yoga, tai chi, or qigong videos. Or simply create your own unique movements. Have fun with it.

31

RANDOM GUIDANCE

Have you ever seen a relevant quote or mantra online at just the right time, and it's as though it was written or posted just for you?

Have you ever found a particular book that called to you, talked to someone who had words of wisdom or insight to share at the perfect time, heard a song with lyrics you deeply connected to, or seen a sign or advertisement that resonated with you, just when you needed it?

These "random" experiences of guidance are often signs from the universe to let us know we're not alone and that our thoughts, feelings, and desires are being heard and responded to.

Sometimes answers or guidance come when we least expect it, and often from unexpected sources. These answers may be to questions we consciously have, or they may be to questions we didn't yet know we had but that we somehow needed. The more open you let yourself be to noticing the messages in the world around you, the more messages you will receive and the more relevant they will be.

The key is to view the world as a place that supports you, not a place to be fearful of. See opportunities and look at things with new eyes. Be open to the wonder around you and let yourself be amazed and surprised. Go about your day thinking, "I wonder what wonderful surprises are in store for me today!" Or, "I'm looking forward to seeing an insightful message in the world around me this week." Then notice what appears, not by consciously looking for it, but by putting the intention out there and then letting it go, knowing that when the message comes, you will recognize it.

When you see a message, ponder over it and think about how it can help your experience of life or a specific situation. Is it calling you to have more faith and trust in the unknown? Is it prompting you to take action of some kind? In some cases, the message may be direct and crystal clear, and in other cases you may recognize it as being important in some way, but it may take a bit of self-inquiry to determine its significance to your situation.

What guidance does the universe have for you this week?

ACTIVITIES

1. As you go about your day or week, be a little more aware than usual. Notice things such as signs, billboards, songs, phrases, advertisements, articles, words people say, or quotes you come across, and jot down or photograph any that feel significant or helpful to you. Note them down in your journal and write a little about what the guidance might be for you.

2. Go to a bookstore or your own bookshelf (or both), and in the self-help or spiritual section, pick up the first book you're drawn to even if you've never heard of it. Open it to a random page and read that page. Does it have a message for you? Don't be surprised if it does!

32

EMOTIONAL FIRST AID KIT

J ust like we have evacuation plans and maps on hotel doors, or first aid CPR charts
for the home and workplace, you can create an emotional first aid protocol and
kit for yourself. Keep it somewhere handy, and have a digital copy too, so you
have access to it when needed.

If emotional upheavals are recurrent, or trauma or mental illness is a part of your
life, also give a copy to your loved ones so they know the best way to help you or to
guide you to help yourself in a crisis, or on a day you may be struggling.

This kit is designed to help you get through whatever you're going through—
not to block or suppress your emotions, but to help you move through them safely
to get to a place where you can function again and then be able to think more clearly
about your next steps.

To make your kit, come up with a plan (or plans, depending on different situations
or simply to have some extra options), written as a list of steps or strategies that are
for emergency use. These steps should include things that can help you stay strong,
survive, and manage what's happening until it passes.

When in crisis, it's easy to feel like it won't end, that there's no way out, that the
feelings will never get better, and that it's too much to bear. You need a way to remind
yourself that the feelings will pass and you can get through it and you WILL feel relief
and feel better again at some point. It's just a matter of riding this wave and allowing
time for it to settle.

Your kit or list can include anything that helps YOU. Anything you feel will
help you get through an acute emotional crisis. This is different from your Joy List,
although it may incorporate aspects of that, but in a more urgent way.

You can also have a physical first aid kit, with things like essential oils, crystals,
music CDs or lists of helpful songs or music tracks, a notepad and a pretty pen,
phone numbers of loved ones who support you, the phone number of a crisis support

hotline, hand cream, an eye pillow, a paper fan, etc. Sometimes just looking at your kit will remind you that you have a lot of support and resources available, and this alone can help you feel better even if you don't use any of it.

Whenever life gets you down, gets too much, or something happens that suddenly shakes you off-center, don't think, "I can't handle this!", think, "Time for my emotional first aid kit." Tell your loved ones to remind you of this, and maybe even create the kit together.

Here are some examples of what could help you:

1. Remind yourself: "This will pass. I'll be okay. Right now I just have to go through this, and I WILL get through it." (Or any other statement of support that feels good to you.)
2. Stop what you're doing and sit or lie down, holding your hands together or on your body in some way, such as in a self-hug, or with your palms on your heart/chest area.
3. Tell yourself, "All I have to do right now is be here and breathe." If you need to cry, cry, but focus on soothing and reassuring yourself.
4. Tell someone. If you're still feeling like things are too hard, tell someone you trust. Text or call them and say, "I'm struggling right now, are you able to help?" Then talk to them and express yourself and let them know what will help. (Listening, coming over, sitting with you, helping to guide you through some strategies.)
5. Refocus. Give yourself another sensation to focus on. Try rubbing your arms gently, or placing a cool or warm cloth against your skin, popping bubble wrap, or cuddling up with a soft blanket.
6. Use music. Put on something that feels supportive and let the sounds wash over you, imagining your emotions being processed.
7. Ask the universe, God, your spirit guides, or any power that you relate to, to help you move through this.
8. Smell a soothing oil like lavender or lemon.
9. Repeat any of the above as needed until the crisis passes.
10. Sleep if you need to. Things often feel much better after rest.

Add any other emergency strategies or tools you like, or a follow-up list to help you transition back to your day, including things such as having a shower, putting on your favorite outfit, making a cup of tea, or sitting under a tree for a while, before getting back into the world.

You might like to keep your list on the fridge, behind the bathroom door, or in a bedside drawer. And save it as a photo on your phone.

ACTIVITY

Create your emotional first aid kit:

1. List of support options and plan of action
2. Physical kit of support resources

What's in yours?
Remember, you've got this.

_____

_____

_____

_____

_____

_____

_____

33

CENTERING JEWELRY

A beautiful way to honor yourself and your center is to give yourself a gift, just like you might give a friend or loved one on a special occasion. In this case, the loved one is you.

I want you to give yourself a gift. Specifically, a piece of jewelry to act as a reminder and conduit for re-centering.

You can do this for free by "regifting" something you already own back to yourself, but with the purpose of it being your "centering" jewelry; or you can purchase a new piece or save up for one: a bracelet, necklace, pendant, ring, anklet, earrings, brooch—anything you'd like. It doesn't have to be fancy or expensive. Whether it's a $10 piece of costume jewelry or a $100 item, it's completely up to you. Whatever you choose, it is the intention behind it that matters most, and that it is something that looks good and feels good to you. It may have crystals or gems as part of it for extra power, but it doesn't have to. It could be a plain piece of silver or something with beads or something you've made yourself.

The only consideration is that this item be purely a reminder to return to center (as well as wearing it for the beauty of it any time you like). Don't choose something that you already associate with something or someone else, such as a wedding ring or an heirloom. Make this piece specific for your centering journey. A physical object can be a great mindfulness tool to act as a point of focus and a trigger for changes in perception and emotion. Your centering jewelry should make you feel good!

ACTIVITY

When you've chosen your jewelry*, hold it and ask your higher self or your spirit guides, or the universe or God, to bless this item with the pure positive energy that is also contained within your center. Ask that simply holding it, wearing it, or looking at it will help shift your vibrational frequency back to alignment with your center. It will also be a reminder of the love you have for yourself and that you are worthy of receiving gifts and pleasure and enjoying beauty.

Wear this piece every day this week to embody this gift and the energy of your center, and then wear it any time you feel like it (even if you're home in your pajamas).

*Don't feel you have to rush to find something. If it takes time to find the right piece, that's okay. Allow yourself to feel a connection to whatever item you choose.

34

PHYSICAL CONSIDERATIONS

While most of this material is about your internal world and shifting perspective through heart, mind, and soul techniques, your physical reality is also important to pay attention to and make adjustments to as needed.

Although changing yourself on the inside often leads to changes on the outside, and we are spiritual beings having a human experience, we can't escape the fact that we are right here in this physical world and also need to look after things from a physical point of view as well.

Many people ONLY look at the physical, trying to change external issues and circumstances without regard for the internal or the spiritual, which often leads to reduced results. Paying attention to both is a more balanced way of looking after yourself and your life experience. What I mean by physical considerations are things like your daily health habits, diet, lifestyle, chemical exposure, exercise, environment, etc. With my background as a naturopath, I've seen many patients get great results from tending to physical considerations, but I've also had patients whose results weren't as good as they could have been, because they struggled with changing their mindset, attitude, self-worth and belief, or other inner issues.

There is also not much point paying a lot of attention to your spiritual self while disregarding or downplaying the importance of enhancing your physical self. So let's look at some options you could consider to maximize your physical experience. Are there any you're not doing, or not doing regularly enough?

* *Get some sunlight every day, but avoid overexposure. Aim for sunlight exposure first thing in the morning to set your body clock and boost your mood.*
* *Spend time in nature often, by the ocean or other waterways, in rainforests, gardens, mountains, the countryside, etc.*

✳ *Walk barefoot on grass, earth, or sand, to help ground your energy.*

✳ *Switch off screens 1–2 hours before bed, or use a screen filter or app that reduces blue light, and wear blue light–blocking glasses after sundown so your body can produce adequate melatonin for healthy sleep.*

✳ *Use candles, salt lamps, or orange or red light bulbs in the evenings to reduce blue light and LED light, which reduce the body's production of melatonin—the hormone we need for sleep, among other things.*

✳ *Reduce overstimulation before sleep to calm your nervous system. Scary movies or books, fast music, television ads, important or difficult conversations are not conducive to sleep.*

✳ *Start your day with a glass of water with fresh lemon squeezed into it. This will help balance your pH and wake up your digestive tract to prepare for breakfast.*

✳ *If you have a family history of memory problems or neurological issues, or want to maximize your brain and slow the aging process, try fasting for 12–16 hours overnight once or twice a week (unless you have diabetes or other health conditions that might be affected by this). This time period allows for two things: a boost of human growth hormone in the morning, and assisting the repair of stressed-out or damaged brain cells and nerves, reducing neurological inflammation.*

✳ *Unless you're a vegetarian, base the majority of your diet around good quality protein (organic and grass-fed meat, chicken, fish, eggs), vegetables and salads, nuts and seeds, and healthy fats like avocado, olive oil, coconut oil, and macadamia oil. Foods like dairy and grains (as well as a too-high intake of red meat) can contribute to excess inflammation in the body which underlies most disease processes, so being aware of your intake is important to make sure most (if not all) of your diet is anti-inflammatory.*

✳ *Invest in a good water filter (unless you have a rainwater tank).*

✳ *Eat "power" foods and spices such as turmeric, ginger, Manuka or raw honey, garlic, fennel, oregano, rosemary, açai berries, dark cacao, and chia seeds.*

✳ *Drink organic brewed herbal teas. Lemongrass and ginger, peppermint, etc.*

✳ *Make healthy soups a regular part of your diet to boost your intake of vegetables, and avoid adding cream or artificial stock powders. You can use bone broth, spices, and Himalayan salt for extra flavor if needed.*

✳ *Make healthy smoothies with fruit, almond or coconut milk, and a little honey if needed. I love making mine with banana, cinnamon, and vanilla.*

✳ *Bone broth or bone broth powder makes a good soup base or something to enjoy on its own to boost the immune system.*

✳ *Invest in a good quality multivitamin and mineral supplement. This ensures you get all the essential vitamins and minerals on a daily basis for energy and metabolism, as your daily diet can vary and often our food supply does not have as many nutrients as it did in the past, due to soil depletion and modern farming methods.*

✳ *Speak to a qualified naturopath or nutritionist about any other nutritional supplements you may need, or herbal treatments that can be beneficial, while also working alongside your doctor when needed.*

✳ *Don't overeat. Reduce portion size and don't keep eating if you start to feel satisfied or full.*

✳ *Reduce chemicals in your diet and lifestyle. This includes food additives, household cleaning products, and personal care products and cosmetics. Source natural alternatives.*

✳ *Reduce clutter in your environment to create more physical simplicity, and less dust.*

✳ *Try to fall asleep before midnight, as earlier sleep boosts immune function, cell repair, and energy.*

✳ *Try a new recipe each week or month to add variety to your diet.*

✳ *Try a different form of exercise or walk in a different area. Try yoga, Pilates, weight training, water aerobics, hiking, dancing, or a sport.*

✳ *Keep your home and office well ventilated and consider adding some indoor plants.*

✳ *Drink only water or herbal tea between meals.*

✳ *Reduce coffee and tea intake to no more than two cups per day, or try switching to herbal, even just for a week to see how you feel. Dandelion tea/coffee is a good substitute for coffee lovers.*

✳ *Take some downtime every day. Whether it's 15 minutes at lunchtime to practice some mindfulness, or a 90-minute sleep, or a 30-minute guided meditation, whatever you can manage to rest the brain and body.*

✳ *When you eat, visualize the nutrients in your food nourishing your cells.*

What other physical considerations can you think of that might help you?

ACTIVITY

Physical changes are best implemented one step at a time. Too much too soon can lead to giving up or going back to old habits. Choose one or a few small changes from the list above to make and implement gradually, and always remember to speak with a health professional if you need more specific guidance suitable for your unique needs.

Be your best self—mind, heart, soul, and body.

35

THE MESSAGE

A valuable skill to learn to help you stay centered or return to center is to understand the secret messages your body is telling you. When you have a physical symptom or an emotional change, unless you need urgent medical treatment, ask yourself what your body needs. Of course, tend to any relief or treatment you may need, but then go deeper. What is this message actually trying to tell me?

Our symptoms are messengers, getting our attention and passing on information we need to restore our equilibrium. Everything is energy, and energy always comes first, so no matter what physical or emotional issue you may be facing, there is always an energetic cause that occurs first. Your body will keep trying to get your attention and pass this message on until you get it, or make a change that shifts the energy.

The more you learn to tune in and talk to your symptoms, and connect with the intelligence of your center, the easier it will become to understand.

To do this, take a few moments to relax and breathe, and become aware of sensations in and around you, then bring your awareness to any areas or issues of concern. With a gentle and honest intention, ask what the message is. What is this issue telling me? What does it need? And how will I tend to that need?

For example, when I became ill with Graves' Disease (an autoimmune form of hyperthyroidism), it wasn't until later that I was able to look back and see what the deeper energetic contributors were. Symptom-wise, my metabolism was going way too fast, using up my nutrients too quickly and leaving me depleted, causing uncomfortable heart palpitations, painful muscle cramps, excess sweating, insomnia, and panic attacks. When I looked back, I was able to see that prior to the onset of symptoms, my lifestyle was speeding up. I was trying to get ahead too quickly and doing too much, staying up later at night to catch up. The thing is, I became subtly aware that this was the case, but I ignored it. I kept going. In the space of one month, I had three wristwatches that broke—one stopped working, on another the numbers all fell off, and on the other the band snapped. The message? Take Time Off. Did I listen? No. And I got sick.

Yes, there are other factors at play in causing disease and symptoms such as genetic potential, environment, diet and lifestyle, infections, etc., but there is always something else going on too, so listen to your body, acknowledge any signs (like the watches), and tend to your needs.

Both physical and emotional issues can give us messages, and we need only ask to find out what they could be.

Here is a general list of body areas and issues that are common, with general insight into what the overall message may be. Yours may be relevant or it may be something different or more unique to your situation:

* *Shoulders/upper back—too many responsibilities, worries*
* *Lower back—need more stability in life*
* *Spine—where are you out of alignment with your true self or your goals?*
* *Hips—two steps forward, one step back. Need to make more progress*
* *Neck—looking to the past too much*
* *Headaches—tend to your inner peace and let go of what you can't control*
* *Ears—listening too much to the opinions of others*
* *Nose/sinuses—negative thinking and excess of toxic thoughts*
* *Eyes—needing to face and accept the truth*
* *Heart—learn to trust life and natural timing*
* *Digestive system—time to focus and make clear decisions, get rid of clutter in mind and environment*
* *Knees/ankles—not being flexible or trusting enough*
* *Feet—not feeling supported. Learn to support yourself better*
* *Hands—sensitivity, needing to protect your energy*

ACTIVITY

Write down any symptoms, conditions, emotions, or issues you experience often, and below each one answer the following questions:

What is it (my symptom) telling me?

What does it need?

How will I tend to that need? (Physically, emotionally, and spiritually)

For example

Headaches:

The message: Stop trying to control external situations and people.

Needs: Peace, reassurance, stability, calm

How: By writing a list of what I CAN control and focusing only on those things. By doing a visualization every day of my ideal outcome. By saying the affirmation, "I trust that all is working out for the best."

_____

_____

_____

_____

_____

_____

_____

36

STEPPING TO CENTER

This lesson is about combining affirmations with forward movement to integrate positive beliefs into your subconscious, to help you become more fully centered.

When you read about moving your energy and creating a centering sequence in previous chapters, you learned how powerful the body can be in triggering a change in your emotional state (and vice versa). The activity of stepping to center is similar, but also works to create congruency between your thoughts and actions, helping you move forward in belief and peace.

To step to center you will need something you can use to symbolize your center—a photograph, drawing, printed image, object, crystal, or just a piece of paper (you may wish to draw a circle on it or write the word CENTER).

Place this item on the ground a few steps in front of you.

Say the three statements of affirmation on the following pages one at a time, and when the first affirmation feels genuinely true for you, take one step forward, closer to center. Then say the next affirmation.

When you've said three different affirmations that feel true to you, you will reach your center, where you will take a deep breath and smile.

If a particular affirmation doesn't feel totally true for you, say the next variation on the list, and if that one also doesn't feel true, try the next one and so on until you've found one that feels right for where your belief is currently, or create your own variation that is similar.

Practice this each day or week, as often as you can, until you can move "up" the list of affirmations and reach a higher vibration more aligned with your center.

After you've reached a comfortable level with this exercise, you can simply step forward once to your center object (or even just take a step forward in general) whenever you need a quick re-center, take a deep breath and smile, as your brain will have rewired itself to a new state of belief. The affirmations will be integrated into your subconscious from your previous practice, and your body will "hear" them automatically through the associated action of stepping forward with intention, without you having to speak (unless you want to).

ACTIVITY

Set down your object to symbolize your center a few steps in front of you. Work through the list of affirmations below and their variations if needed, until you've said three different affirmations that feel true for you.

✲ **Affirmation 1:**

I am worthy of feeling absolutely wonderful.

*If it feels completely true, take one step forward. If it doesn't feel completely true or there is any hesitancy, work your way through the list below until you find one that does:

I deserve to feel good. (Step forward if it feels true, or try the next one below):

I give myself permission to feel good.

I am open to feeling better.

Take one step forward when the affirmation feels true.

✲ **Affirmation 2:**

I love and accept myself exactly as I am.

*If it feels completely true, take one step forward. If it doesn't feel completely true or there is any hesitancy, work your way through the list below until you find one that does:

There are lots of parts of me that I love.

I am becoming more loving and accepting toward myself.

I am open to learning how to love and accept myself.

Take one step forward when the affirmation feels true.

✲ **Affirmation 3:**

I am feeling completely centered right now.

*If it feels completely true, take one step forward. If it doesn't feel completely true or there is any hesitancy, work your way through the below list until you find one that does:

I am well on my way to feeling more centered.
I am in the process of becoming more centered.
I am open to feeling more centered.

Take one step forward to meet your center object when the affirmation feels true.

When you reach your center object, take a deep relaxing breath, and smile. When you've worked your way up the list of affirmations so the first or second feels completely true (this may take days, or weeks), the next time you need to re-center you can just take one to three steps forward, then breathe and smile to represent getting back to center.

37

TOTALITY

The concept of totality is about understanding how the laws of life work and trusting the big picture. We want things to go well in our life and we want to feel good, and that is our right, as life is supposed to be enjoyable. But as life has its ups and downs, we can sometimes focus too much on the downs or become annoyed or upset at them, disrupting our sense of center.

One way to handle these times is to become aware of and remember the totality of life, and in particular the law of opposites.

Many people know about the law of attraction, the concept of like attracts like, but this law works in tandem with the law of opposites. When you set an intention and make the most of the law of attraction by aligning with the vibration and emotions of your desired manifestation, not only do you trigger the process of manifestation, you also trigger the law of opposites, because without an opposite, you cannot know the other opposite. Everything is relative.

When something unwanted appears that disrupts your center, consider whether or not it relates to one of your desires.

If so, it is most likely a manifestation of the law of opposites. These opposite situations or obstacles to what we want occur because of the delicate balance of energy in the universe, and actually show that what you want is manifesting. The opposite will usually appear first, and then your desired manifestation, as long as you get back to and maintain alignment with your desire and do not let the perceived obstacle disrupt your alignment for too long.

It can be easy to feel disappointment when an opposite occurs, not realizing it's actually a positive sign along the journey; but if you can recognize it for what it is, it will be less likely to disrupt your center because you'll be able to see the big picture and know that everything is working out.

If a lot of opposites appear, it may be that your alignment is a bit off, or you are focusing too much on these unwanted situations, thereby attracting more of the same. So not all opposites are a positive part of the manifesting journey. Some are simply from a recurring negative vibration that needs to be adjusted. Being aware and discerning about what's going on at a deeper level is key.

What you resist persists, so instead of pushing against something unwanted when it occurs, what about welcoming it instead? Not in a "Hey, come at me!" kind of way, but an, "Oh hello, I see you there. I know you're here for a reason. I trust this," kind of way.

For example, if you're wanting to manifest a more harmonious work environment, and you set that intention, you might find that your work colleagues start getting on your nerves, or some kind of disruption occurs, adding to disharmony instead of harmony. This serves two positive purposes: it reinforces your desire for a harmonious work environment, strengthening the vibration for this desire, and it shows that the law of opposites is in effect, shaking things up so that your desired harmony can find its way to you and create a balance of energy. It's not up to you to figure out how to try to fix everything. You can do your part, of course, but trust that the universe knows what it's doing. Perhaps it's allowing for a change of staff, or a new opportunity to arise for you to work somewhere more harmonious. Trust the process.

ACTIVITY 1

Write down a few of your main intentions or goals you're working toward, just in simple terms to remind you of your desires, so that if something unwanted occurs you can look at your list and recognize if it is an opposite. If it relates to it, then you can feel relief in the understanding of totality and say, "It's okay, it's just part of the manifesting journey."

_____

_____

_____

_____

_____

_____

_____

_____

_____

_____

_____

ACTIVITY 2

Sit or lie down, well supported, and close your eyes. Notice any areas of pain or tension or unwanted sensations in your body, or any unfelt but known areas of dis-ease or difficulties, and then let your awareness roam until it finds another area *without* that sensation or dis-ease. Notice how the unwanted sensation isn't necessarily encompassing your whole being. So instead of thinking, "I'm in pain," focus your thought on the area that is in pain, and then add the thought that this other area is NOT in pain, that it feels comfortable. This way it takes the pain out of your complete identity, making room for healing and also acknowledging the parts of you that feel good. Even if it's a small part, like an eyebrow, or a fingernail, or your lips. Whatever feels *not* uncomfortable, or feels like it is working well, such as your heart beating or your lungs breathing, bring your awareness to that. Give thanks for that part. Also give thanks for the uncomfortable sensation in the other part that provides the contrast to allow you to recognize the comfortable part. And then alternate your awareness between the two sensations, the uncomfortable and the comfortable, until you can visualize and feel the energy from the comfortable part wrapping around or merging with the uncomfortable part, nourishing it and supporting it and showing it that it's possible to feel good. Working in harmony with these opposites helps create a more loving relationship in your body in regard to any physical issues.

You can also do this for emotional discomfort. Focus on a difficult emotion you're experiencing, and any parts of the body you are feeling this emotion present in, and then either feel your way into the opposite of this emotion, or find an area of the body that doesn't seem to be storing this emotion and focus on that. Know that you are not your emotion or emotions. You are experiencing them only. As with the physical discomfort exercise above, do the same with emotions, alternating between the uncomfortable and the comfortable, allowing the more pleasing emotion to nourish the areas that are feeling uncomfortable emotions, feeling relief in this.

Remember the totality of life.

38

EXPLORE

Discovering new places can nourish your center and shift your perspective to raise your vibration. We get used to the same familiar surroundings and experiences, diluting our awareness. Although familiarity and having a stable environment is important for centering and keeping your nervous system calm, expanding your awareness through the exploration of new places stimulates wonder and prevents energy stagnation. It's like an injection of energy and vibrancy into your center.

Have you ever felt invigorated and renewed simply by going somewhere new or having a new experience? We need this for our expansion and momentum, and to feel more alive.

We tend to travel the same routes, visit the same stores and cafés, or follow the same walking track because we feel safer with what we know. And yet people often book holidays and weekends away to new places, often far away, to explore something different. But it can be good to explore what is already close and accessible to you. How much have you not discovered due to being lost in the familiarity of your comfort zone and safe space?

Expand your awareness through exploration, and make conscious choices to go somewhere different or look at the same thing from a different viewpoint, or delve deeper into a place you already know to see what is new to discover.

To do this, you could try playing tourist and looking up things to do or places to visit in your area. Make a list of places you haven't been and add them to your diary or use it as a checklist to mark off each new place you see. You could call it: **My Explore List**.

Some ideas and examples:

✳ *Visit the national parks near you.*

✳ *Go to a community information center or local museum and learn about the history of where you live.*

✳ *Find the places that have the best views or lookouts.*

✳ *Watch a sunrise or sunset at one of these places.*

✳ *Go somewhere new to swim, walk, run, hike, or have a picnic.*

✳ *Visit a garden or even a plant nursery and explore the different varieties of plants and flowers.*

✳ *Visit a local store you haven't been to before and strike up a conversation with the owner or employee to learn more about their passion or reason behind the business.*

✳ *Explore the posters and signs on a local community notice board and try to look into at least one—maybe a new health or fitness class, a book club, social or support group, music lessons, etc.*

✳ *Drive the scenic route to a destination, even if it takes longer.*

✳ *Visit a different town or city nearby.*

✳ *Attend a community event or fundraiser, or create your own.*

✳ *Park your car somewhere different when you go somewhere you usually go, such as a big shopping center, or town center.*

✳ *Go somewhere you've been before but explore it more deeply and mindfully, by noticing what colors are most present. Are there flowers or plants? Any signs of people being there recently (such as footprints)? What sounds are present?*

✳ *Visit a different or alternative movie cinema you haven't been to.*

✳ *Attend a local theater production.*

✳ *Look at new ways to explore new places; for example, boat rides, helicopter rides, tour bus, train, cycling, history tours.*

✳ *Be a guest in your own neighborhood. If you can manage it, indulge yourself in a night "away" at a local B&B, hotel, cabin, caravan park, or guest house. See your locality from fresh eyes and enjoy the vacation feeling without having to travel far or pay travel expenses!*

Doesn't just thinking about those ideas make you feel more alive and invigorated? We need familiarity for stability, but we also need newness to keep our energy flowing. Remember to occasionally to put on your explorer hat and see what you can discover.

ACTIVITY

Make your own **Explore List**. Add ideas from the list on the previous page or create your own. Draw a checkbox next to each idea, and tick them off when done. Schedule some of the ideas into your calendar or keep some for spontaneous adventures. You can write down a few here to get the process started.

_____

_____

_____

_____

_____

_____

_____

_____

_____

39

VERBALIZE

Talking is one of the most natural things we do each day. But often we don't verbalize what we *really* want to say. Your voice is powerful and a healing tool, and when used more consciously you can help yourself remain in or return to center.

Tell someone how you're feeling right now. Whether it's happy, excited, nervous, worried, or sad. Tell someone. Tell yourself. Tell your journal. And even better, *ask* someone how *they* are feeling. Open up, allow others to open up, and let any facades fall away. Just be real. Hear someone out, understand them, and let yourself be heard too. This is not to dwell on anything negative or uncomfortable, but to simply get the emotions acknowledged in the company of a fellow human being. After that, you might like to do another of the return to center activities; maybe even WITH this other person. You could suggest taking a few minutes for mindfulness, walking in nature, or doing something joyful.

Get used to verbalizing how you feel, what you're intending or wanting, and what you're grateful for, rather than letting your mind go around in circles. Writing things down is powerful, as we know, but sometimes saying things out loud is, too.

When you're upset, instead of huffing and puffing and letting it build up inside, say something out loud. "I feel so annoyed." "I feel misunderstood." "I'm feeling overwhelmed."

Acknowledgment is always the first step in any emotional healing process.

Then say out loud what you want, intend, or wish for. "I want an apology." "I want to be understood." "I want to feel at ease."

This then shifts your focus to what you want, and then you can more easily start focusing on where your power is and what you can control. And sometimes just saying these things out loud helps release some tension and allows you to move through it.

But don't only use your voice during difficult times, use it during positive times too. State how good you're feeling. Celebrate it. Maybe even sing it: "I feel good!" Say why you feel good: "I feel so good because it's beautiful weather today!" "I feel good because I'm doing what I love today!" Or "I feel good just because!"

Say to people, "I feel great today, how do you feel?"

Open up a dialogue, not to fix anything that's wrong or dwell on anything negative or even to boast, but to embrace the wonderful gift of our voice and human connection.

You can also assist this process and embrace your voice by supporting your throat chakra, at the front of your neck, by wearing blue colors, including blue jewelry, and wearing (or meditating with) crystals on your throat chakra such as blue lace agate, blue calcite, angelite, and sodalite.

This week, practice saying out loud what you're feeling throughout the day, positive or negative, and what you're wanting or intending. "I am going to have a wonderful day!" "I am going to take good care of myself today."

ACTIVITY

Right now, out loud if you can, or to someone else, say how you're feeling. You might like to tell them you're reading this book and going through the activities, and this is one of them, and would they be open to being a sounding board as you verbalize a few things?

Over the coming days, practice talking to people and asking them how they feel or what they want. This is not the usual standard greeting of "Hi, how are you?" without really caring about the answer, but genuinely asking how they are *really*, or perhaps asking, "What's been the best part of your day so far?" Or, "What are you looking forward to today?" By doing this you can help not only yourself but others, too. Some people going through difficult times can actually feel worse when people say "Hi, how are you?" because they don't want to focus on how bad they're feeling, or don't want to seem fake by saying, "Good, thanks," when they're not. Rephrasing this question with the above suggestions can help overcome this and give them a more specific question to answer without dwelling on any negative feelings. It can also lead to more meaningful and positive conversation, which can be helpful for both parties.

Happy talking!

40

REMEMBER THE OCEAN

The ocean spoke to me one day. It said. . .

Do not worry, for I am always here.

Do not think too far ahead, for the next wave will come when it's ready.

Do not stand back, step into my waters and feel the life force coursing through you.

Do not be afraid to write on the sand for fear of it being washed away, for I will fill your words with my energy and carry them for you.

Do not fear tension, for it will always release, as easily and fully as my water spreading on the shore with refreshing relief.

Do not think that things have to be flowing perfectly all the time. . . allow for the back and forth, the up and down, the chaos and the calm, and settle into the ebb and flow.

Remember me when life knocks you down.

Remember me when you wonder if you have the strength to get back up.

Remember me when you need a reminder of your own life force, because we share the same energy.

Remember me.

Remember the ocean.

I wrote the above after going through my first miscarriage. I was outdoors, watching the ocean at dusk and trying to handle my emotions. It felt like the ocean was literally speaking to me, and the words flowed quickly. Nature is a wonderful reminder of our inner strength and center, of our connection to our flow of well-being, and our ability to grow, transform, and bloom in adaptation to changing circumstances.

What can nature teach you?

ACTIVITY

Complete any of the following sentences that resonate with you, in your journal. You may like to take a walk in nature first, or look through some nature photos to get yourself immersed in the vibrations of the natural world:

✳ *The trees teach me that. . .* (I don't have to rigidly stand still to be strong. Being flexible but stable in my own strength helps me cope with the winds of change.)

✳ *Flowers remind me that. . .*

✳ *Mountains tell me. . .*

✳ *The sky helps me see that. . .*

✳ *The moon enlightens me to the fact that. . .*

✳ *The sun's message to me is:*

✳ *The stars teach me about. . .*

✳ *The earth beneath my feet reminds me that. . .*

✳ *Air helps me remember that. . .*

✳ *Add any other parts of nature, or animals, that you feel especially connected to.*

See what you can learn from the world around you to help with your centering, like the ocean helped me with mine on a difficult day.

41

NOTHING NEEDS TO BE FIXED

You have all you need within to handle anything in life. It can be tempting to want to fix problems and try to force an outcome, especially when other people are involved and they are not cooperating, but the only things you can control are your own choices, perspective, and actions.

When you understand the concept that nothing in life needs to be fixed, it creates a huge feeling of relief. It also creates trust, because you know that other forces are at play to work everything out and all you have to do is be yourself, be authentic, speak your truth, trust your intuition, and look after yourself, and all else will unfold in the right way and at the right time. This doesn't mean sitting back and letting life happen to you, but just stepping back a little from the control and fixing mindset to one of ease and trust and flow.

Sometimes when you try to "fix" something, it can make it worse or make the problem last longer, because your mind is focused on it being a problem in the first place. A good analogy to explain this is with a skin wound. If you have a cut on your skin, the body's healing mechanisms are immediately activated. It will cause redness, swelling, maybe some pain, and eventually a scab, until the tissues have been repaired and new skin has been formed, which pushes the scab away as it is no longer needed. As long as it's not serious or infected, the best thing you can do is leave it be and let your healing process occur in its own time.

If you think of your emotional wounds in the same way, or any perceived problem or issue as being like that skin wound, and the inflammation and scab as the feelings, then just as you would with the physical healing, let the emotional healing take place and the feelings be felt and acknowledged. Feeling = Healing. If you pick at a wound or try to get rid of a scab because it's uncomfortable or painful or you don't like the way it looks, it's going to make it worse. It's going to take longer to heal and delay everything. It's the same with emotions. If you reject your feelings (the scab) and try to get rid of them instead of letting them form and be experienced and seen, it will delay the healing of the issue. Just know that feelings are moving you through a healing process and don't need to be removed or treated or fixed; they just need to be experienced and witnessed, and supported.

When the scab has gone (or the intense or uncomfortable emotions), it may be completely gone or there may be a scar (physical in the case of the wound or emotional in the other case). At this point there is still no fixing that needs to take place, but you can soothe it and help it to heal further or be less noticeable (by using creams and oils for physical wounds, or self-care and psychological and spiritual strategies for emotional scars).

Feel, don't fix.

Soothe, don't stop.

Let the process and cycles of life resolve things for you, and surrender to the healing and divine flow of nature.

Nothing needs to be fixed, only felt, acknowledged, allowed, and experienced, then soothed and supported. Remember this in difficult situations when your mind wants to take control and fix something, and you will find peace within your center.

ACTIVITY

When faced with an issue you wish could be fixed, try saying, "I don't need to fix this." Or "I trust that this problem is being resolved in its own way and time." And then support your center so that the process of going through difficult times is easier. Don't fight against what's happening in your life. Accept it for now as it is, then shift your perspective and know that when you are centered, life circumstances will shift too.

What are some other things you could say to yourself when you instinctively want to go into fixing mode? Feel free to jot a few down here:

_____

_____

_____

_____

_____

_____

_____

_____

_____

_____

_____

_____

42

RAPID RESET

Have you ever wished you had a reset button you could push whenever things get off-center or just too much and you find yourself thinking, "Oh no, not again" as you fall into that downward spiral of negative emotion? Or when your day does not go according to plan or you find that recurring patterns of reactions happen in response to situations? For example, you promise yourself you won't take things other people say or do personally, but then someone does or says something and you do have a negative or uncomfortable reaction to it.

The key to these sorts of situations, or when things start to go downhill in general, is to first RESET and then RESPOND, instead of reacting automatically from your past experience and conditioning.

Think of the activity in this chapter as your reset button. Your *rapid reset* button. We may not have a magical one, but we can create one in the mind.

You can't reset and go back to change or fix anything, but you can reset your view of it and adjust your next step, helping you to heal or move forward from anything that's happened and return to your center.

To do a rapid reset, follow the suggested steps below, and adjust if needed to suit the situation or environment you're in, or to whatever feels best to you.

1. Choose a part of your body to act as a physical reset button. It may feel silly but it will help your brain recognize what's happening and help the process occur automatically over time with continued practice of the strategy. You could squeeze your pinky finger, rub the back of your neck, give the back of your hand a pat, press your palm against your upper arm, tap the top of your head, or massage the palm of your hand with your thumb. Try some of those out or something different and see what feels right.

2. As you do this gesture, say silently or out loud, "Reset." This is another variation of the verbal commands you learned in an earlier chapter, but this time with a physical cue, and follow-up strategies to assist.

3. Take a deep breath and consciously loosen your muscles, especially around the neck and shoulders.

4. Speak (in your mind or out loud if possible; go to the bathroom if you need privacy) or write down the following: "I feel [this] and I want to feel [this]." This is about acknowledging your emotions before moving forward. For example, "I feel frustrated and I want to feel satisfied." Or appreciated, or at peace, or happy, depending on the situation.

5. Say or write three things you're grateful for or that you appreciate, either in general or about the situation or person. For example, I'm grateful for this chance to gather myself together and return to center; I'm grateful for this beautiful painting on the wall; I'm grateful for the sun shining outside today.

6. Say or write: "What I would love is. . ." or "Wouldn't it be nice if. . ." or "What if. . ." (focusing the possibilities on what you want or desire but without expectation).

7. Repeat what it is from Step 4 that you want to feel, for example, "I want to feel satisfied," or "I love it when I feel satisfied," and then think of something else (unrelated to the person or situation who may have triggered your negative emotion) that makes you feel that particular desired emotion. So, to feel satisfied, you might like to complete a certain task, go for a refreshing walk or a gym class, have a nap or a massage (even self-massage), do a simple drawing, bake something, do a crossword, or read one chapter of a book.

8. Do that thing that brings that emotion to life for you (or schedule time to do so). Focus on and enjoy the feeling it brings. This way you are putting your emotional satisfaction and well-being back in your own hands, in your control, getting your power back, your center back. You may not be able to change a situation or what has happened, and you certainly can't control other people, but you can choose what to do next and how you want to feel, and bring about your desired emotion in another way, which then helps you to attract more things that result in that emotion.

9. Reset complete. Repeat this process as often as needed, or for separate issues or emotions, even if you have to do it several times a day.

As you get used to this process, or for less intense situations, you may find that sometimes all you need is steps 1 to 3 and that's enough to trigger a reset. Otherwise go through all the steps until you feel some relief.

You may also wish to have a dedicated reset journal purely for this process. Or use your phone or send an email to yourself. Writing things out can help the process along, as it also releases emotion and makes things clearer.

ACTIVITY

Try the above process, and whenever things feel difficult or challenging at any time, just remember: **Rapid Reset**. Follow the steps, and keep your center your top priority.

43

MOTHER YOURSELF

Just because we are grown-ups, doesn't mean we don't need nurturing, motherly support from time to time. If you have your mother around and have a good relationship and she can provide this maternal care when you need it, that's great, whether it's simply a supportive hug, chat, or a home-cooked meal, or more.

Or you may have a relative or friend who is highly nurturing. Reach out when you need it and ask if they're able to provide some extra care, and let them know how they can help you best.

Either way, whether you do or don't have someone who can fulfil a mothering role, it is helpful to learn how to mother yourself. To be your own parent, in the way that you need it, or perhaps the way you never got it before, if that is the case.

I know it's not exactly the same as someone being there for you, but if you go deeper as to how being mothered helps you, you can look at ways to give this to yourself.

For example, if being mothered makes you feel secure like you used to as a child, what else makes you feel secure? What else made you feel secure as a child? See what you can do to refresh that feeling and bring it to the surface again. Perhaps lying on a rug on the floor and coloring in a book helped you feel safe and secure as a child. Do some coloring now for yourself. Maybe you had a collection of soft toys that were like friends to you. Find a cute and cuddly soft toy you can snuggle up to when needed. Our inner child still exists in our subconscious mind, since the subconscious is mostly formed in the first seven years of life, and our inner child still needs nurturing.

Maybe another way you felt secure and mothered was being snuggled up on the couch with a blanket and your favorite food or a hot chocolate, reading (or listening to) a book or watching a cartoon. If so, do that. Watch your favorite childhood TV program, or something that helps you feel secure and at home. For me, it would be *Bewitched* and *The Brady Bunch,* or a cartoon like *The Jetsons* or *The Flintstones.*

If being mothered helps you feel accepted and loved, look at ways you can shower yourself with acceptance and love. Write a list of positive attributes you love about yourself. Run yourself a bubble bath. Find a soft toy to cuddle during the night. Don't feel silly because you're an adult—we are all human and we all still have that child inside that needs nurturing support from the divine feminine.

Other ways to mother yourself (and support your inner child) may include:

✻ *Wrapping yourself in a soft and cozy blanket.*

✻ *Singing a soothing tune or lullaby to yourself.*

✻ *Rubbing your muscles or your upper arms.*

✻ *Running fingers through or playing with your hair.*

✻ *Baking yourself a cake or treat, or buying one.*

✻ *Letting yourself know you are always there for yourself.*

✻ *Giving yourself the advice you know you need, and trusting it.*

✻ *Taking yourself on a fun and playful day out.*

✻ *Having a picnic or tea party.*

✻ *Doing some unplanned sketching and doodling.*

✻ *Letting yourself have a restful day in bed or on the couch.*

✻ *Watching feel-good movies.*

✻ *Reminding yourself to go to bed earlier and get a good night's sleep.*

✻ *Having a nourishing home-cooked meal.*

✻ *And also, looking at how you can be a supportive mothering figure to someone else in need. What we give, we receive.*

ACTIVITIES

Answer the following:

1. Being mothered helps me feel these positive things:

_____

_____

_____

_____

2. I can help myself feel these things by: (write a list unique to you, and include any of the above ideas as well).

_____

_____

_____

3. Try a self-mothering meditation by relaxing your body, slowing your breathing, and imagine a soft pink glow rising up from Mother Earth, merging with your heart. Send glowing rays of this pink light to any emotions or physical areas that need a mother's touch. Or to all areas of yourself. Feel your inner child being in a state of complete love, support, and joy. Remember, you are loved and supported.

44

CENTER POEM

I see poetry as a collection of words that are woven together into a succinct and meaningful message to express something, or to reach deep into the heart and soul. It's amazing how a few simple words creatively crafted into a poem can resonate deeply either individually or collectively. Poetry touches on elements of our existence and nature that are difficult to express in other ways, almost like a painting with words, allowing us to have a brief but powerful glimpse into an aspect of life.

Because poetry can have a quick effect and often an emotional impact, it can be useful as a tool for centering.

There are two ways to utilize poetry for centering: You can write poetry in general to help express and center yourself, and/or you can create a center-themed poem to refer back to again and again to remind you of your connection to your center.

When writing general poetry, you may like to choose a topic, or have a visual prompt, or you may like to simply let words flow without any planning and see where they lead. This can be great for those times you're off-center because you're feeling trapped or stuck in some way, giving yourself a few moments of freedom to write anything you like.

When writing a Center Poem—a creatively worded representation or reminder of your center—take some time first to do another centering technique to connect with your center. Then, from this space of alignment, write your poem, using words and phrases that embody what it feels like, looks like, or simply metaphorical expressions that embrace centering to you. There is no right or wrong. It can rhyme but it doesn't have to. You can use flowery language or simple words. It can be short, sweet, and direct, or long and detailed. You might like to give it a title, such as *My Center*, or *The Center*, or simply *Center*, or something different such as *Connected*, or *The Space Within*. You might like to read some examples of poetry first to get you started, or you may prefer not to have any influences and simply write.

Here is a short and simple example of a Center Poem:

Center Power:

> *There is nothing like this feeling of freedom, of calm*
> *It energizes yet settles me like a soothing balm*
> *The magical space inside that is clear yet full*
> *It draws me in with its magnetic pull*
> *It's there when I need it, always loving and stable*
> *It reminds me that I'm strong, calm, and able*
> *I sometimes disconnect and forget my own power*
> *But I can consciously return and bloom like a flower*
> *In life there is always the yang and the yin*
> *But I know with certainty my true power is within*

ACTIVITY 1

Practice some general poetry as a way to express yourself and help you feel calm and centered. Use a topic or a prompt if needed, or simply look out your window and write a poem about what you see, giving it deeper meaning. Your poems can be a few lines long, or even pages.

ACTIVITY 2

Create a special Center Poem that represents your center, and/or your expression of what being centered is all about. You can experiment a few times, delete words, or start again from scratch until you feel good about it. Give it a title if you wish, and perhaps even turn it into a work of art in a special frame to display. Nobody has to read it unless you want them to, so don't hold back—be you and let your center shine!

45

MAKE A DECISION

When you feel off-center, indecisiveness can often result. This puts you in a state of limbo, not knowing which direction to take or what to do next, feeling paralyzed, or perhaps being busy but not productive.

Consciously deciding something in moments like these can not only help get you out of limbo and move you forward, it can even shift your emotional state. This happens by reinforcing in your mind the fact that you have the authority to make a decision and that you are the boss of you. Nothing else has to take control of you. Making a decision, about *anything,* helps you feel empowered and in control of yourself and your day, even your whole life.

The type of decision you make isn't the point of this strategy (see chapter 49 for strategies involving decisions that re-center you). The power here is in the act of *making* the decision. Simply saying with confidence and intention, "This is what I've decided," gives you agency and helps to focus your energy on something specific or on a certain direction or action, eliminating the scattered feeling that often occurs when you're off-center.

So when utilizing this strategy, decide what to decide. Make a decision about anything in that moment and declare it with specificity. It can be related to a goal, or simply a choice between two alternatives. It can be a small decision or a big decision, but I recommend not making significant decisions that will impact your life until you have returned to center, so that you don't act impulsively from a place that is not your best.

Here are some examples of decisions you could make:

    ✳ *Today I'm going to wear a brightly colored outfit.*

    ✳ *I'm going to fill up my water bottle and drink all of it within the next hour to rehydrate.*

✳ *I'm going to go for a walk at lunchtime today.*

✳ *I'm going to unsubscribe from five email lists today.*

✳ *Tonight I am prioritizing my sleep and I am going to switch off all screens at 9 pm and read a book.*

✳ *I will eat two pieces of fruit today.*

✳ *I'm booking myself in for a massage.*

✳ *When I receive my paycheck I'm going to put 10% aside for my health and well-being.*

✳ *I'm going to ask my boss for a pay raise.*

✳ *I'm going to start my new business in the new year.*

✳ *I'm going to read an inspiring book each month.*

✳ *Tonight I'm going to watch a funny movie instead of a scary one.*

✳ *I'm going to ask a friend if they'd like to meet up for coffee.*

ACTIVITY: Make Your Decision

If you are feeling off-center right now, ask yourself, "What can I make a decision about?" For example, if you are getting ready for work, or to attend a social function, you could make a decision about what to wear, clothing-wise or just a small accessory.

If you are at home and don't have anything specific that needs doing, decide on something to do, or decide to rest.

If you are planning your week ahead, make a few decisions in advance relating to your plans so you feel more prepared and empowered.

Right now, I've decided to. . .

Tonight, I will. . .

Tomorrow I'm going to. . .

Next month I am. . .

_____

_____

_____

_____

_____

_____

46

MOMENTS, NOT MINUTES

When we always have our eye on the time or we race against the clock to do as much as possible as soon as possible, we put our nervous system on high alert, which can throw us off-center, physically and mentally. Time is an important construct in society, of course. It helps us structure our day and provide a framework for productivity, but it can also become an obsessive focus for how we spend our days. Although the time on the clock is very important for people's jobs or career (especially for those who are paid by the hour), we all need time in our life when the minutes don't matter, or when we choose to not let them be the priority.

Moments are the antidote to minutes. Moments are what string our life together; a continual flow of experiences rather than segments divided into minutes or hours. Living in the moment doesn't mean not planning ahead or being organized or productive, it simply means seeing the moment as a nonrigid pocket of time and space to allow yourself to be fully present. You can have productive moments, relaxing moments, exhilarating moments, or any type of experience. Living in the moment doesn't necessarily mean you are being 100 percent calm or at peace or having time out. It means you are being mindful of how you are being or expressing yourself in each moment, no matter what you are doing or not doing, living with more purpose and awareness. Moments are integrated into your everyday life, not something you have to take time out for.

So whenever you do not have to be specifically focused on each minute or hour, try focusing your awareness onto the moments in your day not defined by time. You can still pay attention to time constraints to structure your overall day while also embracing the moments. Simply let the time be present in the background while you naturally flow from one moment to the next. This helps your mind and body re-center itself, and when you are centered, you are better able to intuitively recognize when it is time for the next part of your day. The more moment-focused experiences you have as opposed to minute-focused experiences, the more you will be centered and present, and ironically, that is when we are often most productive or time efficient.

How can you find more mindful purpose in each moment instead of racing against the clock?

ACTIVITY

One of the best ways to make the most of moments, interestingly, can be to schedule time for them. In an ideal world we could just let moments rule and run the day, going with the flow, but in society we often need to be more structured in order to have more balance in life and allow for better self-care.

So although it seems counterproductive, write down some days or times when you could make moments your priority. You can have special moments throughout your day, and/or if you have a whole weekend off and to yourself, for example, you could focus the whole weekend on living in each moment and letting them unfold.

For this activity, write down some opportunities in your schedule for moment-focused living, and also write down ideas for how you can either spend your moments, or maximize the enjoyment or awareness of certain moments that are already part of your day.

1. I can focus on being in the moment on the following days/times this month (if needed, set an alarm for when you need to be somewhere or do something specific, so you don't have to watch the clock and feel rushed):

Days and times (Monday afternoon until I need to pick up the kids from school, Tuesday night at my exercise class, Friday lunchtime, Saturday until dinner time, next Sunday at our family gathering, etc.):

2. How I will embrace the moment during certain activities (While at an exercise class, instead of checking the clock to see how much longer there is to go, I will be present and focused on breathing well and visualizing my body becoming stronger):

Activities:

a. _____

_____

b. _____

_____

c. _____

_____

3. What are some ideas for how I could spend special moments of "free time" without worrying about the clock? (Meditating, walking, creating art, talking to a friend without rushing, reading until I feel like stopping, baking, watching a documentary):

a. _____

_____

b. _____

_____

c. _____

_____

d. _____

_____

e. _____

_____

47

SILENCE AND STILLNESS

We live in a busy and noisy world. Both nature and the materialistic world are always moving, creating, and becoming more. We can often get too caught up in this noise and movement, rushing around, trying to get ahead, our dopamine-addicted brains seeking out stimulation, to the point where silence or stillness seems elusive or even strange.

These two experiences are extremely precious and incredibly valuable. If they can be tapped into and embraced, especially together, then great healing, peace, and relief can be achieved in these quiet, calm moments.

Excluding those with hearing deficits, experiencing true silence is rare. It seems there is always some kind of noise in the world around us, even for those who live remotely and isolated. There are beautiful sounds in the world and it is a great gift to be able to hear them—birdsong, the ocean lapping at the shore, a loved one's voice, children laughing, exquisite music. But at times we need a break from all the sounds so we can hear the call of silence and listen to its sweet nothingness. Silence, or as close as possible to it, gives our brain a chance to have a break from the overstimulation of our noisy world, and can help us listen to our own inner voice and soul. When excess noise is making us feel overstimulated or off-center, find a way to bring some quiet or silence into your day. A few moments of silence can be soothing and delicious, so make the most of those moments and listen only to your breath and the callings of your soul.

Here are some ways (both big and small) to bring more quiet or silence into your life:

❋ *Wear good earplugs at night, or any time you wish to reduce noise. Moldable silicon plugs that cover the entrance to the ear canal are very effective, especially for those who can't use foam earplugs or fit anything comfortably in the ear canal.*

* *Headphones, especially noise-canceling headphones, can help too. You can even wear these over the top of earplugs for extra noise-blocking!*
* *Minimize sources of noise that you can control—turning off the TV, or putting your phone on silent, for example.*
* *Visit a quiet place in your area or travel somewhere quiet to spend some time or to have a vacation.*
* *Swim or float in water, as water blocks many sounds. You can also visit a flotation spa where they have special baths at the perfect temperature that you can immerse yourself in.*
* *If your living environment or location is always noisy and this is consistently affecting your well-being, see if you can make a change and move elsewhere.*

Stillness, too, feels rare in today's society, when we are always on the go, and the world around us is moving at super speed. We often feel if we stop that nothing will get done or we will fall behind, or that we are being lazy or wasting time. But too much activity without any space for stillness can do the opposite, burning ourselves out and missing out on the amazing value that stillness can provide to both our bodies and our minds. Stillness helps the body rest, of course, but it also calms the mind. It helps your energy settle and reset, and allows your blood flow and energy to go to where it is most needed in your body. When we are always moving, our muscles take a lot of our energy, and this is a great thing as activity is essential for a healthy life. But time to be still also helps our other cells and organs to receive some extra nourishment, especially when the stillness calms our sympathetic nervous system and activates the parasympathetic nervous system, which is the state that allows for relaxation and healing. Stillness can also be a way to meditate and tune in to your body and become aware of how you are feeling both emotionally and physically.

Here are some ways to bring moments of stillness into your life:

* *Have a daily meditation session where you lie down on a mat on the floor, a couch, or a bed. Lying on the back is best for rebalancing the body, unless it is medically unadvisable for you to do so (for those in later pregnancy, those with heart problems, or certain back or mobility problems, etc.).*

✳ *Sit in a comfortable chair and just be still for a while. Even if there are things going on around you, just breathe and relax.*

✳ *When you wake in the morning, before stretching and rolling over or getting out of bed, be still for a while, really noticing this stillness, and become aware of your surroundings. Mindful stillness is a beneficial way to start your day, followed by mindful movement.*

✳ *Notice when you are fidgeting, or looking for things to do with your hands. Do what you need to do to satisfy this urge, but then consciously allow yourself to be still.*

✳ *Try floating on your back in a calm pool of water so your head is safely above the water.*

✳ *When you are walking around somewhere and not really needing to have a quick pace to be efficient or to exercise, try slowing down. Even slowing down can bring some of the benefits of stillness in a slightly different way.*

✳ *Purposely slow your movements sometimes when doing tasks, just to notice how it feels. And if you can, pause for a while before resuming. Feel the benefit of this stillness.*

✳ *Take a "stillness break" between activities, to help process what you've been doing and to reset and prepare for the next activity.*

ACTIVITY 1

To first appreciate the beauty of sound, if you are not hearing impaired, list as many beautiful, interesting, or joyful sounds in life that you can think of.

ACTIVITY 2

Choose one or more of the ways listed to bring silence into your day, and decide on when and how you will implement them. Note how you feel before, during, and after the moment of silence.

I will bring more silence into my day by:

Before doing this I felt:
During the silence I felt:
After the silence I felt:

ACTIVITY 3

List any times in your day where you can/could have experienced some moments of stillness (while washing the dishes, while shopping).

ACTIVITY 4

Plan a day/time when you can let yourself be perfectly and consciously still for as long as you're able to (excluding sleep).

How I felt during this stillness:

*Note: silence and stillness in some people may trigger or bring up past trauma, because when the mind and body are calm and less stimulated, the brain is more likely to try to process unresolved trauma. This is not necessarily a bad thing, but just something to be aware of. If you are prone to panic attacks or have a history of trauma, make sure you have a support option in place (such as a friend on call, or a plan for something nice you'll do next like have a shower or a cup of tea) before trying the strategies in this chapter.

48

NATURALIZE

When you spend time with nature (naturalize), you not only connect with your own center, but that of the Earth. This has a double benefit for both you and Mother Earth, combining our life force energy and strengthening our overall spiritual connection. When you honor and respect Mother Nature and appreciate her power, you are both giving and receiving a gift. Nature has amazing healing powers. Sunlight helps our body produce vitamin D. Water keeps us hydrated and alive. Oxygen from trees helps us breathe. There are various foods, plants, and herbs with medicinal or nourishing qualities. And there is also the benefit of getting back to simplicity and the beauty of the Earth we live on.

One power that nature has is the ability to always return to center, to reestablish homeostasis. When there's a storm or a fire, nature knows how to adapt, heal, and regenerate—all processes that are essentially re-centering. In nature there can be upheavals, times of intensity or crisis, but there is always calm and strength. We are the same in our own lives. We have intense times. These can be ongoing or can recur more than we'd like or more than we think we have the ability to withstand, but we can always return to calm, to center, when we choose, even if it's only mentally at first. In tough times, remember nature's power and this re-centering ability, and remember that you have it too, because you are also part of nature.

There is more to naturalizing than just going for a walk in nature or sitting on the grass. That is of course beneficial, but there are many more ways to naturalize, depending on how attuned or comfortable you already are with the natural environment. If you've lived in a city or urban dwelling most of your life, depending on the type of location, nature might seem foreign to you and be experienced only in glimpses, like weeds growing through cracks in the pavement, a tree planted along a sidewalk to beautify a neighborhood, a blue sky backdrop behind the tops of tall buildings, sunlight streaming through gaps in buildings, or potted plants within your home. So even a slight increase in your exposure to nature will have positive effects.

If you're already surrounded by nature, then either reducing your screen time or other time spent with technology to spend more time with the nature you have, or simply communing with nature more deliberately and intentionally and looking for new ways to connect, or new places to explore, will be helpful. You may like to spend a screen-free day in nature, or go on a hike or a camping trip. If you're not one for camping or hiking, try a picnic, a fishing trip, swimming, a whale-watching cruise, or picking flowers in the garden. Even sitting against the trunk of a big tree and feeling its support is beneficial. Nature is always there to support and nurture you.

ACTIVITY 1

Find somewhere in nature to sit quietly, or if you can't get anywhere in particular, try looking at a tree outside the window, or simply a potted plant or bunch of flowers next to you. Breathe slowly and notice all the details of nature—the lines, shapes, patterns, colors, textures, and sensations. As you breathe, feel your lungs filling with the same life force that powers nature, visualize yourself as part of nature, and with every breath feel the natural world breathing with you.

What I did:

How I felt:

ACTIVITY 2

Get creative with nature. Go on a natural treasure hunt, collecting bits and pieces from the world around you, as long as you are not in an area where removing items is not allowed. Pick up flowers, leaves, branches, twigs, driftwood, seashells, sand, pine cones, etc. Use your treasures to create a nature display: an arrangement of natural treasures so you have something nurturing to look at, which may be temporary or permanent. You could display this on the center of a dining table (a nice way to symbolize returning to center), on a bedside table, a shelf, in an outdoor garden, or anywhere that feels special. Children can get involved with this too, and it is a great family centering and naturalizing activity to do together.

Items I collected:

What does my nature display symbolize to me?

_____

_____

_____

_____

_____

_____

_____

49

CHOICES

I f you sometimes feel like life is happening TO you rather than FOR you, remember that you always have the power to choose. You can change anything you don't like, whether completely or partly, by choosing differently. At first it might feel like you don't have a choice, and yes, some situations in life can be restrictive or limiting, but there is always some kind of choice you can make for the better.

You could choose:

✻ A new perspective

✻ A new career

✻ A new morning or evening routine

✻ A new way of eating

✻ Who you surround yourself with

✻ Which external factors you expose yourself to (e.g., not watching the news)

Choices give you power for two reasons:

1. You feel more in control, and therefore more centered, because you know you have a choice (see also chapter 45, Make a Decision).

2. You can improve how you feel by making *specific* choices that help you return to center.

When making a choice, ask yourself, "What's the worst that can happen?" and even better, "What's the *best* that can happen?" Consider the positive possibilities rather than just the negatives, or the people you might disappoint.

ACTIVITY

Think about certain situations or areas in your life and how you might improve them or improve your response to them. What choices can you make to re-center physically, mentally, emotionally, and spiritually? For example, in your relationships, you might make a choice to list positive traits of your partner or a friend. This helps you focus on the positive, create an air of gratitude, and help re-center. For your career, you might choose to enroll in a new course or field of study, look for a new job, or start a business doing what you love. For your health, you might choose to eat more vegetables or drink more water, or see a therapist, or make time for relaxation and exercise. For your home, you might choose to move to a new location that better suits your lifestyle choices and dreams. Remember, what's the **BEST** that can happen?!

General life areas:

    Choices to make for my career:
    Choices to make for my relationships:
    Choices to make for my home:
    Choices to make for my finances:
    Choices to make for my physical health:
    Choices to make for my mental health:
    Choices to make for my spiritual connection:

Specific situations in your life that are challenging:

✲ SITUATION A:
I choose to:

✲ SITUATION B:
I choose to:

✲ SITUATION C:
I choose to:

50

CHOOSE A STATE OF BEING

Most people have a *To Do* list of some kind, or a diary or calendar with lists of tasks to do and errands to run. But not many have a *To Be* list. To Do lists are helpful to clarify what we need to do and when, but To Be lists help us in a deeper way—to *do* things from a place of being centered.

This means that you focus on how you want to *feel* or *be* first, and then bring that state into your daily tasks, and/or decide *what* to do based on how you want to be in that moment or in that day. By *being* first, then *doing*, you often end up being more productive anyway or achieving greater results and outcomes. Starting with your center always leads to a natural flow-on effect that influences what you're doing so that you are not doing things from a place of tension, fear, obligation, or frustration. Even if there are things you need to do that you're not enjoying or looking forward to, such as certain job tasks, going through painful procedures, or doing housework, you can still choose a state of being to help you begin that task from a higher level of comfort and awareness, which will give you strength, motivation, and empowerment.

For example:

"Today, I am going to be GRATEFUL." Notice all the things as you go along that you're grateful for. I'm so grateful I found a good parking spot, I'm grateful it's sunny today, I'm grateful the receptionist was so friendly and helpful, I'm grateful my family member is coming with me today, etc.

"During my medical procedure I'm choosing to be COURAGEOUS AND CONFIDENT." Think of times you've felt courageous or confident and believe that you have those traits in you. Know that simply being there for the procedure is courageous in itself, so you are already off to a good start. Try smiling and telling yourself "I'm courageous and confident," or, "I'm supported and safe," or anything that brings you into a state of those feelings.

Create an affirmation to help you remember your chosen state of being and repeat it throughout the day or during a particular task.

So next time you're writing your To Do list, add a To Be list to your To Do list! Coming from a place of being helps you connect more to your center. It can also help to notice the positive states of being in others (instead of their negative ones) and actually tell them, "I love how resourceful you are," or "It's so nice how you inspire others."

ACTIVITY 1

Choose some things from your To Do list and next to them write a state of being you'd like to embrace during that task. Then remember to consciously embody that state, or you may also do a centering technique to bring you into a better frame of mind first to help you embody that state you choose.

To Do: _____

_____

To Be: _____

_____

To Do: _____

_____

To Be: _____

_____

ACTIVITY 2

Create a To Be list, purely because you like feeling those states of being. List several states of being you enjoy or want to feel—just because, not necessarily associating them with any task. Then choose a state of being on a particular day or time and see how things naturally unfold based on your embodiment of that state, and notice the inspired choices you naturally make and actions you take that align with that. For example, "Today I'm choosing to be creative, and I look forward to seeing how many creative opportunities I integrate into my day." This helps you focus your intention not so much on the task itself, but on the state of being that will help you with your tasks.

To Be List:
Creative, Enthusiastic, Helpful, Inspiring, Resourceful, Productive, Amused, Happy.

Your To Be List:

_____

_____

_____

_____

_____

_____

_____

51

DRAW AND COLOR YOUR CENTER

Creativity can be a means for reconnecting with not only your uniqueness and your potential, but also your center. Creativity comes from deep within, *from* your center, in collaboration with your heart, mind, and soul, so by being creative you are accessing the power within and the possibilities that are allowed to come forth into existence through your unique perspective.

Any creative activity is beneficial for centering, but with this strategy you can receive extra benefits by directly utilizing artistic creativity to represent your own center.

If you were to draw your center, what might it look like? If you were to color your center, what type of coloring page are you most drawn to that makes you feel centered or at home when you look at it?

Drawing is a beneficial activity because it also connects us to our inner child, and children are more often centered than not. It gives you a sense of freedom and possibility, which can feel empowering. Empowerment comes from your center.

Coloring is another tool for centering, as it brings the benefits of color therapy as well as mindfulness. Different colors can trigger different feelings in your mind and body, so use colors that feel good. I've made a specific centering coloring page that you can download from julietmadison.com to print out, or you might find another page elsewhere that suits your center more. Follow your intuition's guidance and trust what feels right.

Choose colors that you feel embody your center—bright colors that feel joyful, or perhaps muted blues and greys that are calming. You can choose one or two colors, or multiple. As you color, make the process itself meditative, rather than trying to achieve a perfect picture. Breathe deeply and feel yourself becoming more connected to your center with every stroke of the pencil, crayon, marker, or other form of media. You might like to display your artwork somewhere you'll see it regularly, to act as a centering reminder.

ACTIVITY 1

Draw a few symbols or sketches to represent your center. You can start by brainstorming ideas with a few lines and squiggles, seeing how your pencil feels moving across the page, and then use your ideas to formulate one specific drawing to represent your center. Don't worry if you don't consider yourself an artist—your drawing doesn't have to be perfect or symmetrical, it just has to feel good to you. It might be a simple circle or triangle, it might be a flower with a heart in the middle, it might be some wavy lines like the ocean, or soft and fluffy clouds, or it might be an elaborate design with swirls and stars. Let it be what it needs to be. Use this space to sketch some ideas and draw your center, or use a bigger piece of art paper:

ACTIVITY 2

Download the coloring page from julietmadison.com or find another page that resonates with you, and use colors that embody how you see your center. Color mindfully while breathing deeply and slowly to help you relax and connect to your state of calm. Display your finished artwork if you choose, to act as a centering reminder.

52

CENTER VISION

The culmination of these strategies is the beginning of a new way of living—from the peace and stability of your center. When you live life from your center as often as you can, you move through life with more ease, trust, and enthusiasm. When you feel enthusiasm, a natural creative urge is often initiated. Creativity is one of the core aspects of the divine life force energy that flows through you, for we are all creators in some way or another. You may be naturally creative in an artistic field, or you may be creative in problem solving, or in idea generation, or communication, or any number of different areas. Mostly, always remember that you are a creator of your own life experiences.

So for this chapter I wanted to include something creative and fun to make the most of the energy these strategies have given you. One of my favorite creative tools is using imagery and words, and for this chapter's activity you are going to create an artistic visual representation and reminder of your center, as well as a special and simple mantra that is unique and individual to you, to help carry you onward.

If you are not reading the book in order, I encourage you to do this activity after trying a few of the other centering strategies first over the course of a few days or weeks.

ACTIVITY 1: Mantra

Firstly, I've mentioned many word-based tools such as affirmations, intentions, verbal commands, self-talk, and writing strategies for centering.

Some reminders:

"Return to Center"—a clear and simple way to train your mind to return to that peace and stability within.

"Clear!" or "Cancel!" when you catch yourself overthinking, or reinforcing negative beliefs.

Now, I'd like you to come up with a short and sweet mantra that is unique to you. Something that encompasses being in your center. Something you can say often to yourself to keep returning to center. Write it down several times, as well as creating a small poster with this mantra written on it.

It could be something like:

❋ *I choose to be in my center right now.*
❋ *My center feels amazing!*
❋ *From my center, anything is possible.*
❋ *I am calm and centered.*
❋ *I have all the strength I need.*
❋ *My center is strong, calm, and healthy.*

Get used to saying it as often as possible over the next week, and then whenever you feel you need to, so you can maintain that connection to your center and remind yourself there are strategies available (52 of them!) to use and help you with any challenge, or simply to enjoy just because.

Now get a piece of paper of any size, and either write your mantra on it and stick it on the wall or fridge, or decorate it first with pictures, stickers, drawings, glitter and/or paint. You may also like to incorporate it into your center vision (below).

ACTIVITY 2: Center Vision

An activity I love doing is to create a collage with pictures and words. It's similar to a vision board, but with a more specific focus. For your center, create a simple collage but with limited cut-outs—just one or a few backgrounds or images, plus a few words to create a poetic phrase or statement that embodies the core energy of your center. It can be your mantra above, or something different.

1. Start with a piece of paper or cardboard (A4 or letter size is fine), then choose a background to fill the entire page or most of it. It could be a wrapping paper pattern, a photo of a landscape from a magazine, an abstract design or blend of colors, or a mish-mash of a variety of images to create a background on top of which you can then place other pictures and words. You may also include a few images of things that feel like they belong in your center, such as a soft cushion, a fluffy cloud, rays of sunlight, etc.

2. Next, find and cut out different words or phrases from magazines and catalogues until you have enough to work with. Then brainstorm word combinations to come up with something that makes sense, both in the literary sense and to your center. This is a phrase or mini poem to celebrate your true self, and the power and peace you have within.

3. Glue the words into your chosen arrangement, and if you like, add any extra touches with images or decorations.

4. Place this on your wall or frame it. You can also take a photo of it and use it as a screensaver.

Your mantra is something to help you continue to rewire your brain and induce calm and self-empowerment.

Your center vision poster will act as a visual reminder of your center and will induce positive emotion and self-love.

Having both a visual reminder and a verbal reminder is a helpful way to be consistent with staying centered and making your inner life a priority.

144

* * *

Thank you so much for coming on this journey to Return to Center.

Writing these strategies has taught me so much more than I expected. And through it all I am once again reminded that there is always hope, there is always peace, and there are always rainbows, both in our lives and within us. No one can ever take away our own sense of self and center. Hold steady and stay strong in the knowing of who you are and what you are capable of. You are an amazing, magnificent soul in human form, ready to live the rest of your life with love and confidence.

With love from my center to yours,

Juliet